PANCHAYATS AND THEIR FINANCE

Panchayats and their Finance

M A Oommen
Abhijit Datta

INSTITUTE OF SOCIAL SCIENCES
&
CONCEPT PUBLISHING COMPANY

ISBN 81-7022-568-X

First Published 1995

Published by
Ashok Kumar Mittal
Concept Publishing Company
A-15/16 Commercial Block
Mohan Garden
New Delhi 110 059

Layout by
Institute of Social Sciences
B-7/18 Safdarjung Enclave
New Delhi 110 029

Contents

A Prefatory Note

Panchayat Finance and Issues Relating to Inter-Governmental Transfers 1
M A Oommen

An Integrated Approach: A Constitutional Imperative 1
The Structure of Panchayat Finance: A Broad Picture 5
Functional, Financial and Planning Decentralisation – A Critique of Conformity Acts (CAs) 18
Inter-Governmental Transfers – Some Conceptual and Operational Issues 22
Conclusion 32

Notes & References 34
Tables and Appendices 38

Finance Commissions and Restructuring of Panchayat Finances 55
Abhijit Datta

Rationalising Panchayat Functions 55
Designing Panchayat Finances 58
Down-sizing the Upper-Level Governments 59
Financing Devolved Functions 60
Generic Issues of Fiscal Transfer 61
Central Contribution 62
Future Decentralisation Strategies 63
Panchayats Plan and Finance 65
Fiscal Distortions 66
Panchayats and Non-Plan Finance 67
Debureaucratisation 68
An Agenda For Fiscal Reforms 69
Conclusions 71

Appendix 72

A Prefatory Note

The papers in this volume require a prefatory note for one or two special reasons. For one, as State Finance Commissions came to be established in different states, our Institute had been approached for help and guidance by many a commission. We had constituted a small committee consisting of Professors I. S. Gulati, M.A. Oommen and Abhijit Datta to convene an all-India workshop on the theme of Panchayat Finances and State Finance Commissions to help clarify the issues involved in inter-governmental transfers. In the meantime, the Planning Commission, the National Institute of Public Finance and Policy (NIPFP) and the National Institute of Urban Affairs (NIUA) had sponsored a more comprehensive national workshop covering the entire local finance, urban and rural. We had been commissioned to prepare a paper on Panchayat finance by the Ministry of Rural Development for the Workshop. It was held at Vigyan Bhavan in New Delhi during October 28-29, 1994. The two chapters in this volume are revised versions of the papers originally presented at the workshop by M. A. Oommen and Abhijit Datta, Senior Fellows of the Institute.

We are publishing these papers in response to the innumerable requests we have been receiving.

We are grateful to Mr B N Yugandhar, Secretary, Ministry of Rural Development, Government of India and Mr. Ashok Jaitly, Additional Secretary in the Ministry, who have been lending constant support to the Institute in our research endeavours on Panchayati Raj, for facilitating this publication.

New Delhi
March 1, 1995

George Mathew
Director

A Prefatory Note

Panchayat Finance and Issues Relating to Inter-Governmental Transfers

M.A. Oommen

THE 73rd and 74th Amendments to the Indian Constitution have cast heavy responsibilities on political leaders, economic planners and administrative bureaucracy of the country in a measure much greater than is apparently being realised. This paper is concerned with only one dimension of these increased responsibilities viz. panchayat finances. The objectives of the paper are (a) to review the existing structure of panchayati raj finances, (b) to review the conformity legislations passed by the various state legislatures, with reference to functions and finances of panchayat raj bodies and (c) to outline some of the conceptual and operational issues of inter-governmental transfers with special reference to State Finance Commissions (SFCs) and the tasks facing them.

The paper is organised under four broad heads: (a) An Integrated approach – a constitutional imperative? (b) The existing structure of Panchayat Finance, (c) The functional, financial and planning decentralisation – a brief review of the conformity legislations and (d) the tasks of the State Finance Commissions - some conceptual and operational issues. This is followed by a brief conclusion.

1.0 An Integrated Approach: A Constitutional Imperative?

The basic issue of inter-governmental transfers in the context of the constitutional amendments is one of rationalizing multilevel public finance with multilevel planning and development in Indian federal polity. The transfer of an indicative list of 29 subjects to the three tiers of Panchayati Raj Institutions (PRIs) along with the mandate to the states to "endow the panchayats with such powers and authority as may be necessary to enable them to function as institutions of self government" (243G) cannot be seen independently of Articles 243ZD, 243ZE, 280 (bb) and 280 (c). This raises several questions related to functions, finance, planning and administration which can only be approached in an integrated manner. The proverbial blind man's approach to understand the elephant is most ill-suited in this context for several reasons.

First, given the spirit of the 73rd Amendment, should not a philosophy of decentralisation inform all levels of government, Union, State and sub-state? If so, this implicit assumption may have to be more explicitly recognized and acted upon. Lack of operational clarity in regard to the concept of "institutions of self-government" is an original sin that may have to be remedied. This lacuna may turn out to be dangerous to the dynamic growth of democratic decentralisation in the country. A fresh look at the allocation of functions and finances as between all the three levels of government viz Union, States and substate rather than the latter two only is implicit in the underlying logic of the 73rd and 74th Amendments. No one can deny that the Union government has been spending a large amount of resources, both financial and in terms of personnel, in areas and on subjects which legitimately belong to the states as per schedule VII list II. Moreover, several subjects in the 11th Schedule fall in the concurrent list (e.g. education, rural electrification, social welfare, public distribution system etc.) and do not fall in the exclusive domain of the states. Again, the 11th schedule covers several functions such as those handled by DRDA, District Industries Centre, District Information Office (NIC) etc. which although jointly funded by the Union and state governments legitimately belong to PRIs. There is a clear case for transferring such functions to the latter, of course with the required finance.

It has to be recognised that the centralised planning with its sectoral earmarking and the various centrally sponsored schemes with national guidelines (1994-95 Union budget has an allocation of Rs. 6032 crores for these schemes) have created formidable hurdles to decentralized planning through autonomous electoral institutions. A senior bureaucrat recently noted: "The ever increasing central schemes and centrally sponsored schemes, which many a time are used to distribute political patronage especially during an election year, will run into difficulties with decentralized planning." (S. S. Meenakshisundaram (1994). p. 110). Another distortion is added by the MPs Local Area Development Scheme. Already the MLAs in most of the states have their version of similar schemes at their level. If following their seniors, the new elected members of the Panchayat Raj Institutions ask for their share of local development on a per capita basis, a demand which has a greater credibility, the process of distortion of planning and development will be complete. Can we ignore all these factors while considering Panchayat finances?

Second, the addition of 280 (bb) and 280 (c) clauses to Article 280 assigning some new responsibility relating to Panchayat finances to the Union Finance Commission (UFC) as part of the 73rd and 74th Amendments, is an enabling provision which in a broader sense may be seen as another attempt at rectifying the imbalances of functions and finances in the Indian Constitution. Article 280 (bb) asks the UFC to recommend "the measures needed to augment the Consolidated Fund of a State to supplement the resources of the Panchayats in the state on the basis of the recommendations made by the Finance Commission of the State." The constitutional approval of a three-tier system with elaborate arrangements for periodic elections and the creation of State Election Commissions, SFCs, District and Metropolitan Planning Committees involve additional functions and corresponding financial responsibilities for the states. The need for a permanent apex financial commission to review federal, finance is thus increasingly underlined. Obviously, the SFCs recommendations will have to precede those of the UFC.

Third, the issues raised in the above discussion will be complete only when they are related with the issues of planning and the role of the Planning Commission, District Planning Committees and Metropolitan Committees where relevant. The District Planning Committee which, unlike the National Planning Commission, is a statutory body (243ZD), has the constitutional responsibility to consolidate the plans prepared by the Zilla Panchayat, Panchayat Samitis and Gram Panchayats besides those of urban local bodies and prepare a draft development plan for the district based on area planning. To call a credit scheme like IRDP as integrated rural development and planning is self-deception, to say the least. Some rethinking on the whole process of planning is, therefore, imperative along with considerations of panchayat finances.

Fourth, the process of restructuring multilevel public finance cannot be seen independently of administrative restructuring. There are several parastatals duplicating services which the Union or state governments are doing. Duplication or triplication of administrative costs must be avoided at all cost. It must start from the Union level down the line. The ultimate goal is to work towards an administrative decentralisation along with functional and financial decentralisation omitting vertical, horizontal and parallel structures.

We may conclude this section by quoting somewhat extensively from the first ever all-India report on panchayat finance published as far back as 1963, namely the Santhanam Committee report, which clearly brought out the need for financial and administrative autonomy as well as an integrated policy to build self-governing institutions at the sub-state level. "Each of them (panchayati raj institutions), being mainly an elected body, has to be self-governing and autonomous to some extent. No representative body will be content to be a subordinate agency. Financial resources have to be adequate for the functions allotted to each Panchayati Raj institution. Nowhere in the world can local bodies function without substantial assistance from governments. At the same time, it will detract from the dignity and autonomy of a self-governing institution if it is to be entirely dependent on assistance from above. It is essential for stability and growth of these institutions that they should have substantial and growing resources which are entirely within their power to exploit and to develop. We deem it essential that every panchayati raj institution should have control over its staff whether such staff is appointed by itself or placed at its disposal by the state government... Broadly speaking, the authority of these bodies over their staff should be analogous to that of the state government over its own servants, or others who have been placed at its disposal by the Central government" (Government of India (1963) pp 4-5). If these suggestions had been implemented, probably the constitutional amendment could have been avoided and the task of providing the right sense of direction today would have been easier.

2.0 The Structure of Panchayat Finance: A Broad Picture

This section is intended to throw some light on the structure of panchayat finance and the flow of funds at the various tiers of panchayats on the eve of the 73rd Amendment. Recent data on this subject are very hard to find. We have tried to piece together some secondary and select field study information and draw some inferences from them. We have tried to preface the discussion by bringing together some major features of panchayat finance based on thirteen state studies sponsored by the National Institute of Rural Development (NIRD)[1] covering broadly the first two decades of panchayati raj in India. We have supplemented this wherever relevant by findings from the Asoka Mehta Committee (1978) which is probably a more authentic study of the period. This section covers (a) panchayati raj finance during first two decades, (b) a broad picture of the finances of Gram Panchayats (GP) in thirteen states and Panchayat Samitis in ten states (PS) in 1989-90, (c) some sidelights on panchayat finance based on field studies/reports of select GPs in Himachal Pradesh, Karnataka and U.P, (d) a broad outline of Zilla Parishad finances based on data from select ZPs in Maharashtra, West Bengal and UP, and (e) some general comments based on all these studies.

2.1 Panchayati Raj Finances During the First Two Decades

This section seeks to present a brief outline of the salient features of the panchayati raj finances during the first two decades of PRIs in India.

The resources of panchayati raj bodies of this period generally may be grouped under four broad heads: (1) own resources, (2) assigned revenues, (3) grants, and (4) loans. Own resources consist principally of taxes and fees, non-tax revenues including income from remunerative enterprises and contribution from the public.

The most important taxes levied in different states by the panchayats broadly are: house-tax, profession tax, vehicle tax, tax on agricultural land, pilgrim tax, entertainment tax, tax on animals and the like. Generally speaking, it may be noted that taxes and fees accounted for about one-third of the total income of gram panchayats during the early periods. By and large the NIRD studies indicate that the tax efforts of gram panchayats in all states have been very poor except in Kerala. This may be seen against "the excellent potential of a number of tax sources" for panchayats which remained untapped (see Government of India (1978) p. 108). That the reluctance to levy taxes can even go to a criminal extent is reported by the Narasimham Committee (1981) of Andhra Pradesh where some panchayats, instead of collecting taxes, made it appear through book entries, that taxes had been collected and spent on development works. (see Narayana Rao K. V. et al (1984) p. 18). While criticising gram panchayats for their reluctance to tax, in fairness it may be noted that the enabling legislations in most states were also highly restrictive.

As regards the intermediate tier of panchayat samitis, while some state Acts had not specified any taxation powers for them, some had provided for imposing any tax which the state legislature was empowered to impose. As a matter of fact, the resource-raising powers of the samitis in most states had been confined to cesses and surcharges on taxes like land revenue, entertainment tax etc., and a variety of tolls and fees. By and large, the financial resources of the samitis did not vary from state to state as the functions entrusted to them were almost similar. Basically, the funds of the samitis were block finances which during this period gradually tapered off. Except in certain states like Tamil Nadu, the intermediate tier did not have much financial resources.

Like the samitis, the zilla parishads in most states also had only limited powers of raising taxes. Except the Zilla Parishad in Uttar Pradesh "no zilla parishad had utilised its meagre powers of taxation" (Government of India (1978) p. 107).

Non-tax revenue as a proportion of total income accruing to the various PR bodies differed from state to state. Several State Acts had provisions for vesting in panchayats various properties of the state government like *porambokes*, roads, bridges and culverts, tanks, waterways, unreserved forests, trees on public land, slaughter houses, ferries and other types of communal property. The main item of revenue for gram panchayats in Punjab and Haryana was the income from such entrusted sources.

In addition to the powers of taxation enjoyed by the different tiers of PRIs and the revenues collected from various non-tax sources, state legislations provided for the sharing of certain taxes levied and collected by State governments. Land revenue, cesses on land revenue and surcharge on stamp duty were the principal assigned taxes distributed between the PRIs. Some states like Kerala had given the entire land revenue to gram panchayats. Some of the cesses levied by the state governments were earmarked for education and road building though generally they were subsumed into general revenues and grants.

Despite several other sources of revenue, grants from state governments – a bewildering variety of statutory and non-statutory categories – happened to be the single major source of income for the panchayati raj bodies. This was more pronounced in the case of panchayat samitis and zilla parishads. Most prominent grants were establishment grants, incentive grants, matching grants and equalisation grants. The establishment grants were given to meet administrative expenses especially those arising as a result of the transfer of personnel by certain state governments to PR bodies. The incentive grants were meant to give incentives for unanimous election of sarpanch, agricultural production, collection of taxes etc. Kerala's record of hundred per cent collection of taxes in several years for a majority of gram panchayats needs special mention in this context. The potential of incentives in the form of matching grants could be seen in regard to Tamil Nadu and Maharashtra. These types of matching grants have provided incentives to the PRIs to adequately tap the existing tax paying potential of the rural people.

According to a noted authority on fiscal federalism, "transfer of funds to lower levels of government can be justified on the basis that such transfers can help equalise income distribution throughout the country by reducing inter-regional service and income differences" (Hirsch W. E. (1970) p. 114). This is as much a federal issue as one concerning the state governments. Both the State Equalisation Fund for making special grants to backward districts to minimise the social and economic inequalities between the various districts and the District Equalisation Fund for making specific grants to reduce inter-panchayat disparities to below district level, established by Gujarat state had addressed this vital issue of equity in inter-governmental transfers of resources, almost with the inauguration of Panchayati Raj in the country.

Apart from taxes, non-tax revenues and grants, some panchayats have relied on loans also to promote development works. One NIRD study reports that Madhya Pradesh government gave interest-bearing loans to gram panchayats for creating community property, remunerative assets like shops and markets, fishery development, poultry development etc. so as to increase their income and make them financially viable (Narayana Rao and Srivastava (1982)). Following the recommendations of the Government of India Report (1963), the Uttar Pradesh Government in 1973 and Bihar Government in 1974 established Panchayati Raj Corporations to give loans to panchayats to promote and take up a wide variety of development works in villages (Narayana Rao and Srivastava (1981a; 1981b). These corporations continue to function even today. Kerala experimented with a slightly different institution called the Kerala State Rural Development Board which is active even today in providing water supply schemes, construction of market complexes etc for the panchayats through institutional finance raised by it. (Narayana Rao (1982c).

We have given above a brief outline of panchayati raj finances during the early period of its existence. The intermediate tier which was very prominent during the early years did not continue to enjoy the same prominence despite the creation of the panchayat samitis in many states. The latter part of the period also saw the gradual erosion of the power, functions and finance of the PRIs as the number of centrally sponsored programmes increased reducing the PRI institutions to mere agencies of development activities rather than as active participants.

2.2 Panchayat Finance: A Statewise Picture

In industrial countries, local governments normally account for 20-35 per cent of the total government expenditure and in some countries, like Denmark, their share is as high as 45 per cent. In developing countries, it is usually below 15 per cent (see UNDP (1993) p. 69). But it is estimated that local government expenditure in India as a percentage of total Union, states, and local expenditure was as low as 6.4 per cent (rural sector still lower at 2.9%) in 1986-87 (Datta, A. (1992) p. 180). Going by these figures, the financial decentralisation in India had not been anything to write home about.

Tables 1A and 1B give the statewise per centage distribution of the sources of income of village and intermediate level panchayats for 1989-90. We have worked out the per panchayat income as well as the per capita income (receipts) and the latter as compared to the statewise per capita receipts (revenue and capital) for 1989-90 to give some insights into the nature and level of decentralisation almost on the eve of the 73rd Amendment. Table (1A) shows that per capita income of gram panchayats ranges from 48 paise in Madhya Pradesh to Rs. 53.22 in UP. UP and Andhra Pradesh figures are exaggerated as they contain JRY grants also. (As reported by the Asoka Mehta Committee (1978), UP Gram Panchayats (GP) had the lowest per capita income in 1976-77 (61 paise). (See Govt. of India (1978) p. 280)).

The average income per GP ranges from a very low Rs. 1,299 in Madhya Pradesh to over Rs. 6.8 lakhs in Kerala. No wonder, the ratio of per capita GP finance to per capita total state receipts in Madhya Pradesh is very high (see table 1A). Here, it may be noted that the average population of a gram panchayat of MP is 3,000 and of Kerala over 25,000. Given the large range of functions assigned to gram panchayats by the state governments, a low average income may be considered as a situation of mismatch of functions with finance. The Santhanam Committee Report of 1963 mentions Rs. 1,500 as a minimum income to support the smallest basic unit. Assuming this figure as valid for the smallest basic unit and allowing for a 10 per cent annual rate of inflation, it would be around Rs.20,000 in 1989-90 to which year the average data under discussion relate. Out of the 13 states mentioned in table 1A, at least four do not make the grade even by this reckoning.

Table 1A also gives the broad pattern of the sources of income of gram panchayats.

To understand the broad headings of table 1A, a brief discussion of the sources of income of panchayats seems to be in order. Generally speaking, the major resources of panchayats of this period may be grouped under six heads. They are explained below.

(1) Taxes and cess assessed and collected by the state government and apportioned to the panchayats. Taking West Bengal as an example, land revenue, cess on roads and public works, cess on minerals, cess on coal etc. fall in this category.

(2) Taxes, tolls, rates, fees etc. assessed and collected by the Panchayat itself, land and building tax being the most prominent.

(3) Grants by the state government for (a) establishment, maintenance of assets created etc. and (b) implementation of assigned schemes including those assigned by the Union such as centrally sponsored schemes. Grants from the state government are of a wide variety such as general grants, specific grants with or without matching conditionalities, establishment grant, incentive grant, equalisation grant and so on. Specific grants are given for construction and maintenance of roads, school buildings, culverts, maintenance of minor irrigation schemes and also for public health and social welfare measures. Several governments give incentive grants for increasing agricultural output, increased collection of taxes, and in some states even for the unanimous election of Sarpanch. West Bengal has an elaborate system of incentive grant tied to the collection of all state taxes and even of small savings from each Panchayat area. From 1989 onwards, West Bengal has given small savings collection to Panchayats with the incentive to retain 50 per cent of funds collected above a set target to form a Development Fund. Rajasthan has an interesting scheme of rewards and punishment related to grants which they call 'Puraskar' and 'Namaskar'. Several state governments like Gujarat and Maharashtra have been giving grants to backward panchayats. There is thus an elaborate grants scheme to finance panchayats in India.

(4) Institutional finance. Though it is not a common feature, panchayats do borrow from financial institutions. UP and Bihar have Panchayat Finance Corporations with contributions of capital from PRIs, the state government and public finance institutions. These corporations give loans for investment activities of Panchayats on a very wide range of items, as we have noted in section 2.1.

(5) Income from assets owned by Panchayats like land, running of remunerative enterprises, etc.

(6) Public contribution. This is a relatively ill tapped source.

It is pretty clear from Table 1A that grants form the major source of panchayat income. The high per capita receipts of UP, Rajasthan or Andhra Pradesh do not mean much given the extremely large grant component of their income which, in the case of Rajasthan, is as high as 95 per cent and in that of U.P, 87 per cent.

Table 1A also throws some light on the Panchayats' performance in the sphere of taxation. The contribution of taxes to total income ranges from 0.9 per cent in Punjab to 63.4 per cent in Kerala. The tax performance of Maharashtra, Tamil Nadu and Gujarat, though it does not cross the 50 per cent mark, has been relatively high. Tax sharing, which is an indication of the states' readiness to promote financial devolution, is conspicuous only in Tamil Nadu (of course as judged by the relative scenario seen in Table 1A). GPs in Madhya Pradesh, Punjab and Haryana, which have a poor record of tax effort, raise the major share of their income from lands vested with them by the state governments.

Thus, the statewise picture shows an extremely variegated scenario.

2.2.1 *Panchayat Samiti (PS) Finance – A Statewise Picture of Sources of Income*

The intermediate tier did not exist in many states. The structure of the sources of income of this tier for 10 states for 1989-90 is given in table 1B. The average income of a block tier ranges from Rs. 82,000 in Madhya Pradesh to about Rs.10.9 million in Gujarat.

The striking dominance of grants is visible in table 1B. The proportion of grants ranges from 6 per cent in Rajasthan to 100 per cent in Orissa. In Andhra Pradesh, it is as high as 96.64 per cent and in Tamil Nadu 81.14 per cent. Gujarat, which has the highest average income among the states under study, obtains 74.73 per cent of its income from grants. Interestingly enough, Madhya Pradesh, which has a poor tax record at the GP level, (Table 1A) raises over 96 per cent of its income from taxes and fees at the block level.

2.3 Some Sidelights on GP Finances Based on Case Studies

This section tries to present more specific insights on gram panchayat finance based on some field studies in Himachal Pradesh, Karnataka and U.P.

The Himachal Pradesh, study relates to the flow of funds in Bankala gram panchayat of Sirmaur district during the entire Seventh Five Year Plan period from 1985-90 (See Arvind Kumar Pande (1994)). Bankala, a GP with less than 4000 population, spent Rs. 69.18 lakhs during the Seventh Plan. Out of this, the panchayat's own resource was hardly 0.50 per cent, whereas about 92.6 per cent came from the government as department schemes and less than 7 per cent by way of institutional finance. The expenditure pattern shows that 44 per cent was spent on rural water supply, 31 per cent on minor irrigation whereas primary health received a negligible 0.25 per cent and primary education and adult education together less than 2 per cent. Apart from the major finding of the study based on a stratified random sample survey of households that the plan priorities did not reflect the felt needs of the villagers, especially of the poor, the author concludes: "The study shows that the finances at the disposal of the gram panchayat are far too meagre for it to discharge its functions. This is due to its own hesitation to levy and collect taxes due to the fear of becoming unpopular. It is thus solely dependent on government for grants-in-aid" (Anand Kumar Pande (1994) p. 275).

The second study, which is based on eight Mandal Panchayats of Karnataka chosen on a multistage random sampling basis, could be considered fairly representative of the state. It covers a five year period from 1987-88 through 1991-92 (See Aziz A (1993a)). In Appendix A, we have presented the sources of income and pattern of expenditure of the 8 Mandal Panchayats to give a broad picture of Panchayat finance at the village level in Karnataka. The average income per year of the eight Panchayats for five years (See Table 1 of Appendix A) works out to Rs. 4.1 lakhs without JRY grants and Rs. 5.5 lakhs with JRY grants. That the tax income of a panchayat (Hinkal Mandal) can go up to Rs. 30.8 lakhs (see Table 1 of Appendix A) and that its total average income without JRY grant works out to Rs. 54.3 lakhs is a story worth reporting. That the tax income of these eight panchayats rose at an average rate of 105 per cent and non-tax revenue by 118.7 per cent during the five-year period, though it may be due to the semi-urban character of some of these panchayats, cannot be ignored in the emerging scenario of panchayat finance. It may also be noted that the proportion of tax and non-tax revenue to the total income even with JRY grants is over 50 per cent. As early as 1989, a Finance Commission of Karnataka noted: "In certain Mandal Panchayats where the pradhans were resourceful and active, substantial revenue could be collected from these various sources in spite of a disincentive to collect due to the restrictions placed on spending the money collected by them by the various rules and regulations in force. We also found that in many Mandals where large scale industrial units were located the panchayats found it difficult to collect from them the taxes which were due to them and which would have improved their resource position considerably." (Government of Karnataka (1989a), p. 120). This shows that fiscal autonomy at the lower level is not a totally unworkable proposition. (If a unit raises over 50 per cent of its income we may say it is fiscally autonomous).

The expenditure pattern (omitting JRY grants) based on the average of seven out of the eight Mandal Panchayats is given in table 3 of Appendix-A. Table 4 of Appendix A gives the pattern of the JRY expenditure of these Panchayats. By and large, more than two thirds of the expenditure has gone to civic amenities and public works. Expenditure on development items is below 1 per cent in two years although the overall average is a little over 2 per cent. As may be seen from

Appendix-A Table 4, 53.6 per cent of JRY grants was spent on public works as against the JRY norm of 25 per cent. These excessive "building" activities add to the burden of maintenance which could not be easily met. This results in poor quality of service and poor productivity and waste of resources. The undue emphasis on public works leads to increase in spillover schemes and cost overruns which tie down free funds available for the future. In all the Mandals as well as in the JRY pattern, SC, ST schemes have been a casualty as the 20 per cent target has been invariably observed only in its breach.

The situation of 11 GPs in the Saharanpur district of Uttar Pradesh (See Appendix B) shows a slightly different picture. For one thing, the average income of panchayats, even including JRY, is very low. Excluding JRY, it is as low as Rs. 21,925 in 1992-93 and including it, it jumps to Rs. 96,750. JRY grant is nearly 3.4 times the total income raised by the Panchayats. The situation tells a somewhat different story from that of Karnataka. That tax income has increased steadily over the years, however, may be seen as an encouraging sign.

2.4 Finances of Zilla Parishad (ZP)

This section tries to throw some light on Zilla Parishad finances based on a general study of Maharashtra followed by a case study of Murshidabad ZP of West Bengal and reference to some other field reports.

The financial resources of Zilla Parishads may be broadly classified under two heads:

(1) *Own Resources*: These include resources raised by the ZPs through levy of taxes, cess, fees etc., besides non-tax resources.

(2) *Grants*: These include (a) assigned resources, (b) Government grants for transferred schemes and for meeting establishment costs and (c) grants for agency schemes.

Table 2 presents the relative importance of the free resources of Maharashtra ZPs vis-a-vis government grants over the period 1980-81 to 1988-89.

The predominance of government grants and the extremely low contribution of ZPs' own resources are well illustrated in Table 2. The sad part is that the level of self-raised resources has declined over the years from 5.9 per cent to 4.1 per cent. The free resources of ZPs in Maharashtra, including freely usable grants and own resources, are shown in column 7 of table 2. It is clear that the "free" grants of the government did improve the situation. Yet, the proportion for most part of the period hovers around a low 7.4 per cent. This indeed shows that fiscal autonomy of the ZPs has been very low.

In Appendix-C table 1, we present the micro situation of the sources of income of Murshidabad ZP of West Bengal. The picture of the internal resources of the district is pathetic with the tax and non-tax resources being as low as 1.28 per cent in 1992-93. The worst part is that the share of internal resources has been on the decline as it was 2.7 per cent in 1990-91. Table 1 in Appendix-C shows that assigned work, including JRY grants, appropriate the lion's share, as high as 94 per cent in 1992-93. The district plan component has shown a drastic decline from Rs. 114.3 lakhs in 1990-91 to just Rs. 28 lakhs in 1992-93.

The situation of Murshidabad may be viewed in the context of the growing decline of untied funds to ZPs (see Table 2 Appendix C) which have been an important aspect of the decentralised planning of West Bengal. The extremely poor resource effort of panchayats[2] at all levels, the declining importance of untied funds and the overarching place of JRY grants go to show that the importance of autonomous decentralised planning in the state has been on the decline. This inference is also supported by what two eminent evaluators appointed by the West Bengal Government have noted: "Wherever we went and whichever panchayat level we met, we were only told of activities undertaken under the Jawahar Rozgar Yojana (JRY). So pervasive is the JRY fixation that in the event of the scheme being withdrawn, the panchayats would have little to do and may have to fold up. That, at least, is the view expressed by some of the panchayats we met". (Mukarji and Bandhopadyay (1994) p. 217).

Not only in West Bengal, in some states like UP, the proportion of district sector outlay itself has started declining from nearly 30 per cent of the plan outlay in 1983 84 to 20.8 per cent in 1993-94. In the districts in the plains of U.P. the decline has been still sharper, from 27.4 per cent to 17.7 per cent during the same period. (See U.P. State Planning Institute, (1994) p. 523). Even in this low per centage share, the free resources available for the ZPs to do independent planning have been insignificant. To cite the Saharanpur ZP's experience, the share of the ZP's own resources mobilised was around 12 per cent of the district sector in 1993-94. This is not integrated with the district plan (See Mahi Pal (1994).

Similarly, it is interesting to note that out of a total plan outlay of Rs. 920 crores in the Karnataka State Plan in 1988-89, a year which saw the Karnataka decentralisation at its best, the share of the district sector was only Rs. 239 crores or 26 per cent. Even out of this, only 14 per cent was freely available to the ZPs to do their own planning. Eighty six per cent of the outlay was on committed items like salaries, matching outlay for centrally sponsored schemes, minimum needs programme, spillover works, etc., (see Aziz, A. (1993)). This dichotomy itself is the negation of planning, not to speak of the low proportion of the free resources at the disposal of the Zilla Parishads. In Andhra Pradesh, the funds channelised through PRIs have been as low as 6 per cent. (See J. M. Girglani (1994) p. 68).

In concluding this section we may offer certain general comments. Broadly speaking, we may say that the panchayat finance at all levels in most states is in doldrums though there are significant exceptions. Tax efforts have been by and large unimpressive, tax sharing minimal and incentive schemes met with only indifferent success. It may also be noted that despite all the records of poor revenue performance, there are clear evidences to show that fiscal autonomy is not an unworkable proposition.

Grants, notably JRY grants, dominate the scene of panchayat finance. Under such a regime of granter-grantee relationships, very little autonomous development and self-rule can happen. The proportion of free resources available to Zilla Parishads for own planning has been extremely low in Maharashtra, Karnataka, West Bengal and UP (states with good track record in decentralisation) and the situation may be worse in other states. Under a grant-dominated financial regime the promotion of fiscal discipline and fiscal autonomy will be simply impossible.

Public contribution, which, in the days of the Community Development Programme, ranged from 34.9 per cent during the First Plan to 40.8 per cent in 1956-57 (RBI Bulletin quoted in Maddick H (1970). p. 126) has not been fully tapped by most Panchayats with notable exceptions like West Bengal Panchayats. The saga of people building over 1000 primary schools and even a truckable wooden bridge (and maintaining it by a Beneficiary Committee which collects the tolls) are important examples from West Bengal (narrated to the author by the West Bengal Minister for Panchayati Raj in a personal interview). The exciting story of the maintenance of two clusters of tube wells, created as part of the IDA projects in the Nayantara and Shyamali GPs of West Bengal, covering 223 acres of command area, by 362 farmers (94 per cent being small and marginal farmers) throws up lessons for the whole of India (for details see Budhadeb Ghosh and Arabinda Ghosh (1992). The contributions of Kerala Sastra Sahitya Parishad (a voluntary organisation) as well as the Centre for Earth Sciences (an autonomous body) in preparing resource maps for village panchayats are other significant instances of public contribution. Public contribution is an expression of people's participation which is the real basis of meaningful local government.

The issue of sustained maintenance of assets, except probably in West Bengal, has not been properly attended to. A quick evaluation study conducted by the Planning Commission in 1991-92 in 10 states shows that 56 per cent of the assets created under JRY schemes were of poor or average quality and the JRY guideline to set apart 10 per cent of funds for maintenance has not been observed. A field study conducted by the Institute of Social Sciences in some UP villages illustrates the tremendous waste of soil conservation schemes, created under the Million Well Scheme, for lack of maintenance causing damage to agricultural production and productivity (see Mahi Pal (1994)). For want of a nail, a battle may be lost. SFCs may have to address themselves to the issue of creating quality assets and their sustained maintenance and may have to evolve useful norms. While several norms from the days of the famous Rafiq Zakaria Committee (1963) are available for the maintenance of municipal services and assets, nothing is available in regard to the assets of the Panchayats. The SFCs may have to address questions such as these in evaluating financial requirements as well.

3.0 Functional,Financial and Planning Decentralisation – A Critique of Conformity Acts (CAs)

This section briefly comments on the distribution of functions and finances of the various PR bodies based on some of the Conformity Acts (CAs). By and large, CAs have been an exercise in amending existing Panchayat Acts for the sake of it to satisfy the mandatory provisions of the 73rd Amendment.

First, a comparison of the functions and powers of GPs, PSs and ZPs, given in a Government of India publication of 1966 and reproduced in Henry Maddick (1970), with those of about 12 CAs which we have studied shows that those in the latter are a continuation of the existing functions with more development works, poverty alleviation schemes, welfare of weaker sections etc. added to the list.

Even a casual look at the number of functions as between the various tiers as mentioned in the CAs shows that a heavy load is placed on the village panchayats without adequate administrative, financial and technical support. In most of the CAs, management and maintenance of assets is the responsibility of GPs. What Maddick (1970) said 25 years ago is probably more relevant today. "The concentration of functions is perhaps greatest in the lowest tier of the system where finances and administrative personnel are invariably in shortest supply"(Maddick (1970) p. 107).

Second, the traditional distinction between obligatory and discretionary functions in many PRI legislations of the past is missing in most CAs. The West Bengal Act is a significant exception as it provides for the implementation of both obligatory and discretionary functions by providing finance and threatening punitive measures for non-implementation of obligatory functions. This is one way of ensuring basic functions at the village level.

Third, in order to ensure clarity, efficiency and proper accountability, a differentiation of functions into essential, assigned and agency categories would have been useful. Whether civic amenities, primary education, primary health care, drinking water supply or employment guarantee scheme or any other should be an essential function and to what level it should be assigned will have to be clearly spelt out by the legislature. Not only that there is no such clarity, the basic principle that whatever can be done best at a lower level must necessarily be done at that level and at no upper level, has not been respected and adhered to. Making primary education, adult education etc the primary responsibility of the ZP (e.g. Himachal Pradesh) is an illustrative case in point.

In the interests of evolving a healthy, stable and sustainable local government in the Indian federal polity, the state legislatures may do well to undertake a detailed examination and review of the various schemes and programmes and transfer as many of them as possible to the PRIs at the appropriate level. Most CAs have chosen the easier method of listing the subjects in the Eleventh Schedule, a strictly legalistic posture. Needless to say, very little will be passed on in practice under such an arrangement. For effective decentralisation, the law itself should list the specific activities under each subject that could be passed on to the various panchayat tiers. As many of these activities are governed by specific state legislations (e.g. education, electricity, water supply etc. etc), they also have to be suitably modified to facilitate the transfer as well as effective functioning of the new regime.

Fourth, in most CAs, (e.g. M.P., Maharashtra, A.P. Karnataka, H.P., Sikkim) functions can be assigned or withdrawn by an executive fiat. Section 312 of the Karnataka Act says that the government may, by notification, amend any of the three schedules for the three tiers. This is clearly against the letter and spirit of Article 243G of the Constitution. To add insult to injury, the functional lists in most Conformity Acts are prefaced by such provisos as "so far as gram panchayat fund allows" (M.P., H.P.) or "subject to availability of funds" (Haryana, A.P., Punjab, etc.)

Fifth, before we comment on finance, some important positive provisions also may be noted. Though there is considerable overlapping and lack of clarity in the allocation of functions, it may be noted that some states (e.g. Gujarat) do provide necessary functions and powers to the Panchayats. Judicial functions have been given in some states like Bihar, Punjab and H.P. The Gujarat Act provides for the creation of a State Council comprising all presidents of ZPs to be presided over by the Panchayat Minister. Many of the problems relating to functional, financial and planning decentralisation could be settled by dialogues and creating conventions through such councils. As in the old Karnataka Act (1985), if the Council had the Chief Minister as its president, its efficiency would have been much higher. Some CAs (e.g Gujarat, Maharashtra) provide for a District Equalization and State Equalization Fund to provide grants to backward villages and districts, a measure, as we have already noted, which the Union also may consider in the interests of distributional equity in the country as a whole.

Sixth, turning more specifically to financial devolution, according to Article 243H, the states have to empower panchayats to levy taxes, tolls, fees, cess etc. besides arranging for tax sharing, grants-in-aid and other measures to enhance their financial capabilities. In the CAs under study, 26 taxes, 24 fee items and five rates have been suggested at the GP level by 12 states. The number of taxes suggested ranges from three in Karnataka to nine in UP, and fees from two in Tamil Nadu to nine in West Bengal. The most common taxes are those on property/building, profession, vehicles and land. It may be noted that Punjab and Himachal Pradesh provide for a specific poll tax on adult male labour to help construction of utilities in a village with the interesting provision to commute it in labour. While most states have given taxation powers to the PSs and ZPs, only a few have specified the taxes and duties. Here, too, Gujarat tops with specifying seven taxes at ZP level and six at PS level, besides several cesses and rates. Tax sharing notably land revenue, is a source of income for PSs and ZPs in several CAs. Some Acts (e.g. AP) provide for sharing of fees. By and large, most CAs have not come up with liberal tax assignment to the PR bodies (Gujarat may be an exception) and most taxes and fees have been of traditional varieties. Innovative taxes and non-tax items are conspicuous by their absence. Generally speaking, there is no effort to match, even remotely, functions and finance.

Presumably, the whole exercise has been left to the State Finance Commissions which is not an enviable task.

Seventh, in most of the CAs, there is provision for concurrent powers of taxation by the different tiers (e.g. Haryana, HP). Such an omnibus provision as that the Panchayats can impose tax on any item within the competence of state legislature (e.g. HP), besides raising innumerable problems such as getting government sanction and conflicts among PRIs, offends the canon of certainty. Budget-making in such a situation also will be difficult.

Eighth, almost all CAs provide for the approval of budget estimates by the panchayats. But most of them do not provide for autonomous budgeting by Panchayats. In AP, no PRI has power to draft or approve budget as it is left to the executive officers of the three tiers. In the Rajasthan Act, the budget of the GP is to be sanctioned by the PS and that of the ZP by the state government. This is against autonomous budgeting and principles of self government. The higher layer authorities may advise but the sanctioning power should remain with the concerned panchayat. In Madhya Pradesh, everything relating to budget is left to the rule making authority. All these suggest that we are still in a pre-73rd Amendment regime.

Ninth, loans (including loans from state government) and borrowing are provided as a source of income in several Acts. The Gujarat CA provides for a District Equalization Fund for loans to village panchayats. The 73rd and 74th Amendments do not make any reference to loans and borrowing except the implicit reference to the various types of available resources which the District Planning Committee may consider for financing the plan (243ZD (3)). But two questions almost automatically come up: (a) borrowing for what? and (b) what should be the format of the annual financial statement? The answer clearly is that borrowing must be for productive purposes and that the usual distinction between revenue and capital accounts also needs to be made in the budget estimates of all levels of PRIs.

Tenth, it is clear from Article 243ZD that a prominent place is given to area planning as against sectoral planning at the sub-state level. As we have already shown, it is also a constitutional imperative that the drafting of a district development plan is part of a bottom up exercise. Clearly, planned development at the district level in the future can be achieved only by some reorganization of vertical departmentalism. The experience of the pre-Amendment regime (where ZP had only an insignificant share of total planned outlay at the district level) has to be systematically reversed by a process of decentralized planning which is but spatial planning par excellence. The Gram Sabhas can indicate their needs and priorities. The GP can identify the lack of facilities in the villages, locate the gaps in services and point out the existing mismatches. Such a lack and gap identification exercise and a simple need-based plan integrated with it can help to prepare proper local level plans.

Most of the CAs, in fact, do not contain adequate provisions for the devolution of powers and responsibilities for preparation of plans and implementation of schemes for economic development and social justice as enjoined in the Amendments.

4.0 Inter-Governmental Transfers – Some Conceptual and Operational Issues

The emergence of the PRIs as a third tier of government throws up anew several issues of inter-governmental transfers in the Indian federal polity. The State Finance Commissions as well as the Union Finance Commission have to address the issues squarely. Even a permanent Finance Commission (membership reviewed every five years) at the federal level appears as a desirable idea as we have noted in section 1.0.

All the CAs faithfully reproduce Article 243I of the Constitution which indicates the tasks expected of the SFCs. Most of them do not care to use 'any other matter' clause. In this section we try to review (a) the tasks of SFCs vis-a-vis the UFC, and (b) some of the conceptual and operational issues arising from the explicit tasks required of the State Finance Commissions by the Constitution. Before that, we may outline briefly some basic principles of inter-governmental transfers with special reference to local bodies in India.

Though a neat matching of functions or expenditure responsibilities and finance or revenue raising capabilities of the various tiers of government in any federal set-up is extremely difficult, some measure of parity is needed besides adequate built-in provision for reviewing and rectifying the possible mismatches. To begin with, the Indian federal set up inherited a yawning mismatch which the statutory UFCs have failed to rectify and, in the process, have even permitted themselves to be hijacked by other non-statutory agencies like the Planning Commission. The tragic part is that even under the new dispensation following the 73rd Amendment, there has not been much serious effort to maintain some measure of vertical fiscal balance in the division of functions and finance at the Union, State and Sub-state level. There is much ambivalence and mismatch at the PRIs level, the nature and magnitude of which varies from state to state, thus making the task of the State Finance Commissions more difficult. It is here that the question of evolving relevant principles and norms of transfers assume significance.

Some basic principles governing these transfers in the Indian context may now be mentioned. Most of them are interrelated. All the same, each SFC may have to review and even spell out the expenditure responsibilities and revenue assignments at each tier in a district as well as the state to ensure some measure of vertical balance.

First, the traditional 'gap filling' approach pursued by the Union Finance Commissions of the past may be irrelevant and even problematic as a method of transfers of finance to the PRIs.

Second, an integrated view of the panchayat finance is needed. The distinction between plan and non-plan outlay must not be pushed too far. If maintenance of projects completed earlier (e.g. primary school, primary health care centre, minor irrigation projects etc) is part of the so called non-plan activity and hence is not adequately taken care of, it is the local people who suffer most. The CAARD Report (1985) pleaded for treating all basic services and anti-poverty programmes invariably as plan schemes (see Ministry of Agriculture (1985) p. 37). The Tenth Finance Commission categorically disapproves of what it calls the "artificial classification of expenditures between plan and non-plan and the attitude of regarding all non-plan expenditure as of low priority" (Report of the Tenth Finance Commission (1994) p. 6). All the same, it needs to be emphasised that the distinction between revenue and capital account must be clearly maintained. Panchayats must enjoy the freedom to borrow (raise loans) in whatever manner they choose to fund capital expenditures. The District Planning Committee may do well to prepare a shelf of viable projects that can be loan-financed. All borrowings will be supplementary to any capital grants they may receive from State or Union government.

Third, economic efficiency and equity which are basic considerations in fiscal transfers must be kept fully in view in regard to sub-state level fiscal transfers as well. Clearly, some degree of inter-panchayat equity has to be ensured. This presupposes some measure of inter-state equity to which the UFC has to address itself. The known failures in this regard have to be reviewed along with the role of the Planning Commission and other fund transferring federal government agencies. We maintain that the federal government has an added responsibility to ensure a fiscal transfer system that ultimately equalises net benefits at least in regard to basic services throughout the country (which in a way strengthens the case for a permanent UFC that reviews the situation periodically and exercises vigil).

Net fiscal benefits as far as possible should be equal across localities. Needless to say, endowment of regions and, therefore, the fiscal capacity to bear the burden of the services and social needs differ widely across localities. In regard to basic services, a rule of thumb criterion is to work out a normative per capita expenditure and deduct a sort of the ability of the PRI concerned in per capita terms to finance the service concerned; then the Union and state transfers must be such as to equalise the benefits to the various local areas. The Union government may have to set eligibility standards. This is because all citizens will have to be treated equally regardless of their place of residence. Everyone should be assured of a certain minimum level of services. This becomes all the more important under the new liberalised regime which is likely to bypass poor people and poor regions. To deprive an individual of adequate level of schooling, drinking water, health and other basic services because of his residence is to do him an injustice. In fact, a major concern of the PRIs should be to ensure certain comparable basic services to the community of citizens they are called upon to serve. Over a period of time, the goal of fiscal transfers should help to facilitate this on a planned priority basis so that each gram panchayat has comparable levels of basic services at reasonably comparable levels of fiscal burden (taxation). This is the best way to ensure some measure of horizontal equity given the wide difference in population size, resource endowments and taxable capacity of regions.

Four, fiscal discipline and fiscal autonomy must be underlined. While fully endorsing the prime responsibility of the federal government for ensuring a certain level of national minimum in the localities that fall within them, the idea of shared responsibility encompassing all levels of governments will also have to be recognised. There must be some fiscal responsibility and autonomy at all levels. Resource-based fiscal management rather than expenditure based budgeting should be the key to fiscal autonomy and discipline. Fiscal discipline has to be related to a well articulated scheme of rewards and punishment. Revenue efforts as well as economy in expenditure have to be rewarded in the same way as profligacy as well as proven violation of expenditure norms have to be punished. At any rate, there should not be any incentive for fiscal mismanagement. Postponing evils by carrying deficit forward to future budget years is a tendency to be checked and some measure of balanced budgeting may have to be insisted upon.

Fiscal autonomy cannot be built in a regime of grants-in-aid. The PRIs can play genuine role in local development and self-rule only if they enjoy some degree of fiscal autonomy. This attribute is clearly more than relying on untied funds and rests on innovative resource mobilisation, including project-tied loans, public contribution and the like. Tax assignment with clear taxing powers, and tax sharing assume significance in this context.

Five, a few other aspects that are important in inter-governmental fiscal transfers may also be noted. They are predictability, transparency and tax coordination. The timing, frequency and the amount must be known in advance to enable the receiving unit to do proper budgeting and planning. They should not be left to executive decisions but should be made transparent through the budget documents. Tax coordination to ensure some measure of inter-state equity in the distribution of the tax incidence as well as inter-state and inter-district rationalisation in the rates of commodity taxes needed particularly in view of the possibilities of competitive taxing, tax rating, tax concessions, etc. to attract investment from potential firms and entrepreneurs by the states and PRIs are more relevant now than ever before.

The operational criteria of inter-governmental transfers may vary from state to state. Ensuring minimum standards of basic services, and providing for basic human resource development functions, correcting glaring differentials in fiscal capabilities and promoting some long-term policy goals such as infrastructural development, removing poverty etc, are important considerations in this regard. Tax-sharing and grants are the two explicit fiscal instruments for inter-governmental transfers provided for in Article 243I. In what manner and in what proportion they should be combined is an operational problem the SFCs have to address themselves.

4.1 The SFCs and the UFC

The tasks of the SFC are very onerous compared to that of UFC. It has no beaten track to traverse or established guidelines to pursue. It has to cut its own path and create its own conventions and traditions. In the aggregate, the SFCs have to face about 500 ZPs, 5000 PSs and nearly 2.5 lakh GPs unlike the UFC. To enhance their credibility and acceptance the SFCs have to stay equidistant from the pressures of the State, the substate level tiers and the bureaucracy.

The UFC as well as the SFCs have a greater responsibility to live up to the letter and spirit of the Constitution than ever before. Though technically the Tenth Finance Commission (TFC) was not governed by the sub-clauses 280(bb) and 280(c) added subsequent to its appointment, the Commission has recommended an adhoc per capita grant of Rs. 100 per rural population (based on 1971 census figures) for the period 1996-2000. The state-wise distribution of this adhoc grant is given in Appendix E. These allocations are meant to be only as an "additionality over and above the amounts flowing to the local bodies from state governments. They should draw up suitable schemes with detailed guidelines for utilisation of grants" (TFC

(1994) p. 48). SFCs can help a great deal in drawing up these guidelines. TFC, by and large has favoured a wider divisible pool and a greater progressivity in the transfers of funds to the states. This is a right signal to SFCs in carrying forward larger financial decentralisation to the PRIs down the line.

The majority of the states do not generate any substantial balance from current revenue. M. J. K. Thavaraj (1978) noted several years ago: "A starving mother like State Government cannot ensure the financial health of the local bodies" (Thavaraj M. J. K. (1978) p. 634). Eight of them in 1994-95 had an estimated revenue gap of over Rs. 6,077 crores. The constitutional requirement of raising taxes under nine heads as per Articles 268 and 269 remains unmet despite persistent memoranda by the States and reminders by experts. Though Estate duty and tax on railway passenger fares had been imposed they were subsequently abolished. The proceeds of income tax which is the only tax to be mandatorily shared with the states (with 85 per cent of it being shared with the states till recently, the Union probably has a lesser incentive to tax and greater incentive to levy surcharges which are not shareable), as a proportion of the total revenue of the Union, States and Union territories have fallen from 21.4 per cent in 1950-51 to 6.1 per cent in 1990-91, part of the reason being taking of the corporation taxes away from the divisible pool. This decline is being mentioned to drive home the need for an objective review of the tax efforts of all tiers, Union and States by the UFC, and the States and lower tiers by the SFCs. Fiscal discipline which means economy in expenditure and optimisation of revenue efforts is the essence of multilevel public finance. The UFC and SFCs, in their periodic review of the country's finances, may have to make objective studies in order to bring out factually the need for discipline at all levels of governance.

4.2 The Task of Reviewing

One of the tasks of the SFCs is "to review" the panchayat and municipal finances. A question may be raised whether a SFC should think of a rural-urban proportion of the divisible cake. The two separate Amendments and the growing rural-urban disparity in basic services and income (A recent study of 1991

Census data by the Census office is indeed revealing. The rural-urban gap in per capita GDP is as high as 3.5 in 1991 (See Planning Commission (1994)). These are valid arguments in support of dividing the divisible pool into rural urban components. But a strict rural-urban dichotomy is unwarranted in this context as a rural-urban continuum has to be promoted as part of the spatial planning exercise in a dynamic growth setting. However, the rural urban gap as a ground reality cannot be missed by SFCs and will have to be taken into account in their scheme of devolution.

Each SFC may have to review its conformity legislation in the light of the 73rd and 74th Amendments with reference to finance. They definitely will have to identify the mismatches in functions and finance and recommend corrective measures via more allocations of funds and recommending matching powers. But this is easier said than done. For one, the question of fiscal adequacy and autonomy has to be addressed if PRI bodies have to be developed into institutions of self-government. The preponderance of grants and the preponderance of sectoral schemes can create big problems. How far this situation may be permitted to continue during the next five years and what are the prospects of bottom up spatial planning may have to be examined in answering the question of adequacy and autonomy. For the first SFC, the question of considering a bottom up district plan can only be notional as PRIs in many states are yet to settle down and the inauguration of the real process of planning as envisaged in 243ZD may take some more time. It can now proceed only on some normative basis. Girglani's (1994) suggestion that a national policy should be evolved to allot 40 per cent of resources as untied plan funds from the total plan allocations for district schemes to be selected through a bottom up district planning process is worth examining in this context. (See Girglani J.M. (1994)P.69). The *inter se* distribution among the ZPs and tiers below them can follow a variant of the Gadgil formula as was followed in Karnataka. Fifty per cent weightage in the Karnataka formula was given to population and the other fifty to indicators of backwardness so that backward districts get a relatively higher share of resources compared with developed districts. A certain proportion of the plan funds allotted to ZPs was earmarked for distribution among Mandal Panchayats (Karnataka before 1993 had only two tiers), based on a similar formula but highly restrictive in regard to the variables of backwardness used. The variables chosen and the weightage for them in the formula should be relevant to the concerned State. What is appropriate for Karnataka may be irrelevant for Kerala or Bihar or Rajasthan. Probably, the federal government may have to review the entire scheme of financial devolution (the case for a permanent UFC which we suggested already assumes greater significance on this score) to see that the net benefits to localities are equalised through the various schemes of Union and State fiscal transfers.

4.3 Tax Assignment and Tax Sharing

As per Article 243I the SFCs have to recommend the principles of tax sharing and tax assignments besides the principles of grants-in-aid. We have already indicated some of them in the beginning of this section (4.0). Taxes assigned should have a local character like the property tax, entertainment tax and land revenue. Though taxes are admittedly a compulsory payment without any direct *quid pro quo*, taxes that satisfy the benefit of service principle will be suitable candidates for local taxation. Further, some measure of linkage between the decision to incur expenditure and that to raise resources should be promoted to encourage fiscal discipline at the local level.

As regards the UFC, tax sharing is restricted to income tax and excise. There is no such restrictive provision as regards the states in the 73rd and 74th Amendments which can be taken as a green signal for a liberal tax sharing if the state so chooses. This gives added advantage or handle to those states which would like to provide greater horizontal equity as between rich and backward panchayats. Probably, SFC has a greater role in this regard. They may do well to choose whether a broad tax sharing or individual tax sharing should be followed.

Each SFC will have to identity the ideal tax/taxes relevant to its state for purposes of sharing in case they do not think of the entire tax revenue pool. A SFC can even impose a surcharge or cess, preferably on a tax showing buoyancy, to be given exclusively to PRIs.

Once the divisible share is arrived at, each SFC has to work out the *inter se* distribution formula for ZPs, PSs and GPs and possibly work out the percentages for each one of them. Here the distribution formula should be based on tax effort and a composite index of backwardness which could be some variant of the Gadgil formula (as suggested in section 4.2) with a lesser weightage to demographic factors.

4.4 Grants

As for shareable tax, for grants also each SFC will have to evolve its distribution criteria. As a blanket suggestion one can say that all human resource development functions such as education, health, drinking water etc. should be grant tied. Here too, each SFC has to work out its own pattern. There is a case for matching grants as against block or unconditional general grants as it may induce greater fiscal discipline. As a well known authority on fiscal federalism observes: "Economic theory, supported by a number of empirical studies, finds that categorical, matching grants induce a significantly larger budgetary response than non-matching, lump sum aid". (Wallace E Oats (1991) p.100). While in principle one may approve of this, a universal application of this can turn out to be injurious to several PRIs which are located in poor or remote areas. Moreover, panchayats that are better able to take advantage of the matching provisions usually obtain more than their proportionate share of the Union/State funds, leaving their poor counterparts worse off than before the programme for which the grant has been meant. The distributional implications of all categories of grants, therefore, may have to be properly evaluated.

4.5 Measures to Improve Panchayat Finances

We have already seen in (Sect 3) that the CAs taken together have an imposing list of over 26 taxes. There are an equal number of fees as well. Two questions are important here: one is the poor base and the second indifference in imposing taxes. The non-tax revenue sources ranging from license fees on animals to sale proceeds from dust, dung and dirt, are also not important sources of income. We have already noted that GPs are generally reluctant to impose taxes on the people they face every day, especially when they fail to show results, and are lax in collecting taxes and do not mind the accumulation of arrears. However, the reasons for the poor performances of local bodies need study along with the remarkable record of several panchayats as we have noted. Are the failures due to poor economic development, poor tax base, lack of adequate tax collection machinery, poor tax rate, poor valuation of properties, collusion and corruption between households and officers etc? All these aspects need further study. The success stories and stories of failure of Panchayats within a state itself are good candidates for case studies. (The SFC can even sponsor short studies.)

There is great potential for raising non-tax income by assigning more land to Panchayats. In a few Panchayats in West Bengal the yield from social forestry on waste land works out to several lakhs of rupees (reported by the West Bengal Minister for Panchayats in a personal interview). Creation of permanent assets like shops, flats, fishing ponds, raising of nurseries and other economic activities are important sources of finance.

Income from agriculture is a legitimate tax source for Panchayats. The states may do well to tap this source fully for the benefit of Panchayats. The table in Appendix D needs no elucidation. The share of revenue from agriculture (including land revenue) for all states as a per centage of total tax revenue has fallen from 10.9 per cent in 1965-66 to 2.6 per cent in 1987-88 and to a negligible 1.18 per cent in 1993-94 despite bumper agricultural harvests during the latter period. Though West Bengal has a comparatively creditable record after 1982-83, its absolute performance too has declined. Haryana's contribution has fallen from 6.6 per cent in 1975-76 to 0.1 per cent in 1987-88 and still less to 0.08 per cent in 1993-94. The message is loud and clear.

Economy in resource use is a factor that is seldom appreciated. If assets created do not survive a monsoon it is a waste of resources. Expenditures that cannot be justified in terms of their avowed goals or realised outcome must be scrutinised. Incremental budgeting as a norm should be dispensed with at the lower tiers. A system of continued review of expenditure items may have to be introduced through a zero base budgeting or through a performance budgeting exercise. In this context, the practical suggestions of the CAARD report for improving the budgetary process and Demand for Grants are worthy to be tried out at least on an experimental basis (Ministry of Agriculture (1985) Chapter V and Annexures V-B to V-E).

It is worthwhile examining the performance of the Panchayat Finance Corporations of Bihar and UP functioning from 1974. The fact that they made profits all these years has to be specially noted. A study of these corporations may provide helpful lessons as regards the question of replicating such corporations in other states.

Above all, people's contribution is a great resource. We have already referred to its immense potential in mobilising resources and maintaining assets. Voluntary agencies also can play a useful role as also educational institutions. In the future a civil community's need may be best met by the community itself. There is also a fast growing rich community in rural India. They can contribute by buying rural debentures/bonds etc. for worthwhile projects issued by Zilla Parishads and create quality hospitals, schools, shopping complexes etc. among their people. An interesting study of the Philippines has empirically established that primary schools that are financially accountable to the communities they serve are more cost effective and responsive to students and parents than the highly centralised public elementary school system with several layers of bureaucracy (See Emmanuel Jimenez *et al* (1988).

5.0 Conclusion

To conclude, the principle of decentralisation should inform all layers of governance and the process of its implementation must be approached in a holistic manner. The lack of an operational meaning of the concept of "institutions of self-government" has come in handy for the detractors of decentralization. The functional and financial devolution have been more to satisfy the letter of the law than keeping to the spirit of self-government. Clearly the new third-tier institutions should be far removed from the post-office style of functioning that characterised them in the past. While inter-governmental transfers may be governed by such broad principles as adequacy, autonomy, fiscal prudence, predictability and transparency, operationally, tax sharing tax assignment and distribution of grants-in-aid *inter se* must be based on criteria which each SFC must evolve, preferably with the help of some composite index of backwardness and measures of resource effort. However, we may have to travel far beyond fiscal federalism in moving towards the goal of building institutions of self government. This can be achieved only if the transitional tasks are pursued with clarity of purpose and dedication to the cause of democratic decentralization, and finance is made to play the inevitable midwifery role in this task. Ultimately, just as India is a union of states, states should be a unions of districts and districts unions of sub-district level panchayats. Finance is a necessary, though not a sifficient one towards realising this task.

ACKNOWLEDGEMENT

I wish to acknowledge the help of Dr Mahi Pal, Dr S N Mishra and Mr N Rajagopal of the Institute of Social Sciences and of Dr B D Ghosh in the preparation of the first draft of the paper.

NOTES

1. These studies are made by Narayana Rao K V (1982a), (1982b), (1982c), (1983), Narayana Rao K V and and Srivastava K B (1981a), 1981b), (1981c), (1982); Narayana Rao K V and Naidu N Y (1981a) (1981b), (1981c) (1981d), Narayana Rao K V, Sastry R K and Vittal C P (1984).

2. The Audit Report of Panchgram, Nabagram and Muhrool GPs for 1988-89 says that the internal resources of these panchayats were 6.7%, 16.2% and 12.7% respectively, a poor record indeed.

REFERENCES

Aziz A (1993) *Decentralised Planning: the Karnataka Experiences,* Sage Publication, New Delhi.

Aziz A (1993a) *Decentralised Governance in Karnataka: The Mandal Panchayat System,* Institute of Economic and Social Change Bangalore.

CMIE (1990), *Basic Statistics Relating to Indian Economy,* Vol. 2 States September 1990, Bombay.

Datta Abhijit (1992) "Local Government Finances: Trends, Issues and Reforms" in Amaresh Bagchi *et al* (1992) *State Finance in India,* Vikas.

Ghosh B and Ghosh A (1992), *On the Path of Self-Reliance:* The Case of Operation and Maintenance of Tube Wells by the Beneficiaries of Two Villages, State Institute of Panchayat, West Bengal.

Girglani J.M. (1994) "Financial resources of Panchayati Raj Institutions" in Amitava Mukherjee (1994), *Decentralisation: Panchayats in the Nineties*, Vikas.

Government of India (1963), *Report of the Study Team on Panchayati Raj Finances*, Ministry of Community Development and Cooperation, New Delhi.

Government of India (1978) *Report of the Committee on Panchayati Raj Institutions,* Ministry of Agriculture and Irrigation, New Delhi.

Government of Karnataka (1989) *Report of the Zilla Parishad and Mandal Panchayat Evaluation Committee,* Dept. of Rural Development and Panchayati Raj, Bangalore.

Government of Karnataka (1989a) *Report of the Finance Commission for Zilla Parishads and Mandal Panchayats*, Government Press, Bangalore.

Hirsch Z. Werner (1970), *The Economics of State and Local Government* McGraw Hill, New York.

Jimenez Emmanuel et al (1988) *Does Local Financing make Primary Schools more efficient: The Philippines case* World Bank working papers.

Maddick Henry (1970) *Panchayati Raj: A Study of Rural Local Government in India,* Longman.

Mahi Pal (1994) Impact of Jawahar Rozgar Yojana on *Employment Generation and Capital formation in the Rural Economy of Saharanpur District*, Institute of Social Sciences (under publication), New Delhi.

Meenakshisundaram S. S. (1994) *Decentralization in Developing Countries,* Concept Publishing Company, New Delhi.

Ministry of Agriculture (1985) *Report of the Committee to Review the Existing Administrative Arrangements for Rural Development and Anti-Poverty Programmes* (CAARD), Department of Rural Development, New Delhi.

Mukarji Nirmal and A. Bandopadhyay (1994) "New Horizons for West Bengal Panchayats (A Report for the Govt. of West Bengal) In Amitava Mukherjee (1994) ed., *Decentralization: Panchayats in the Nineties,* Vikas.

Narayana Rao, K. V (1982a) *Finances of Panchayati Raj Institutions in Gujarat*, NIRD, Hyderabad.

——— (1982b) "Finances of Panchayati Raj in Orissa", *Journal of Rural Development*, Vol. 1, No. 6.

——— (1982c) "Panchayati Raj Finances: A Study in Kerala", *Journal of Rural Development*, Vol. 1, No. 5.

——— (1983) "Finances of Panchayat Raj Bodies in Tamil Nadu" *Journal of Rural Development*, Vol. No. 1.

Narayana Rao and Naidu N. Y (1981a), "Management of Panchayati Raj Finance in Maharashtra", *Behavioural Science and Rural Development*, Vol. 4, N0. 1.

——— (1981b), "Panchayati Raj Finances in West Bengal", *Rural Development Digest*, Vol. 4, No. 2

——— (1981c) "Finances of Panchayati Raj Institutions in Bihar," *Rural Development Digest*, Vol, 4, No. 4.

——— (1981d), Panchayati Raj Finances and their Management in Andhra Pradesh", *Rural Development Digest*, Vol. 4, No. 1.

——— (1981e), "Panchayati Raj Finances and their Management: A Study in Rajasthan", *Rural Development Digest*, Vol. 4, No. 1.

Narayana Rao, K. V. and Srivastava K. B (1981a) *Rural Industries: A Study of Panchayat Udyogs in Uttar Pradesh*, NIRD, Hyderabad.

——— (1981b) *Panchayat Raj Finance Corporation in Uttar Pradesh and Bihar*, NIRD, Hyderabad.

——— (1982), *Panchayati Raj Finances in Madhya Pradesh*, NIRD, Hyderabad.

Narayana Rao K. V., et al (1984) *Mobilisation of Resources by Panchayati Raj Institutions in Andhra Pradesh*, NIRD, Hyderabad.

Oates Wallace E. (1991), *Studies in Fiscal Federalism*, Edward Elgar.

Pande A.K. (1994) "Flow of funds in Panchayat Benkala during the Seventh Five year Plan" *Journal of Rural Development*, Vol. 13 (2), NIRD.

Planning Commission (1994) *Background Paper on State Urban development Strategy*, Housing and Urban Development Division, New Delhi.

Ranganathan V, (1992) "Analysis of Finances of Zilla Parishads in Maharashtra", *Panchayat Raj Institutions, July 1992.*

Report *Tenth Finance Commission* (1994).

Reserve Bank of India Bulletins, April 1992 and February 1994.

Thavaraj M. J. K, (1978) 'Finances of Local Governments in India', *Indian Journal of Public Administration,* Vol. XXIV, No.3.

UNDP (1993), *Human Development Report, 1993,* New York.

UP State Planning Institute (1994), *Decentralised Planning in the State: District Level Experiences* (Hindi), Area Planning Division.

Table 1A

A Statewise Percentage Break up of Income of Gram Panchayats and Per Capita/Per Panchayat Receipt of States (1989-90)

Sl. No.	States	Taxes of fees (%)	Remunerative Enterprises (%)	Revenue from lands (%)	Share of revenue (%)	Matching grants (%)	Grants from Govt. (%)	Govt. loans grants for creating remunerative assets (%)	Other income (receipts) (%)	Per capita income (Rs)	Average per panchayat (Rs)	Per capita receipts of states (Rs)
1	2	3	4	5	6	7	8	9	10	11	12	13
1.	Andhra Pradesh	13.61	1.32	-	6.59	0.03	78.43	-	0.03	40.60	101145	856.79
2.	Goa	41.15	1.22	-	-	2.89	20.62	3.06	7.18	28.38	107022	2892.73
3.	Gujarat	30.99	-	0.82	2.82	0.94	41.01	-	23.42	27.56	56053	1193.41
4.	Haryana	13.16	-	61.57	-	9.31	1.92	-	14.04	10.90	23363	1241.11
5.	Himachal Pradesh	6.93	-	-	1.36	3.58	7.52	0.85	79.77	9.68	17593	1763.17
6.	Kerala	63.40	1.23	0.14	-	-	14.45	-	20.78	31.43	684702	984.44
7.	Madhya Pradesh	-	-	92.14	-	7.86	-	-	-	0.48	1299	753.71
8.	Maharashtra	45.24	-	-	6.48	-	25.24	-	23.04	12.01	22706	1268.47
9.	Orissa	5.57	3.93	2.71	-	-	85.31	0.30	2.18	2.39	14942	877.18
10.	Punjab	0.99	-	33.86	1.06	-	50.89	-	12.25	26.42	34465	1446.77
11.	Rajasthan	-	-	4.94	-	0.09	94.97	-	-	40.37	186103	820.65
12.	Tamil Nadu	33.31	-	-	31.82	-	34.87	-	-	3.12	8651	1003.19
13.	Uttar Pradesh	1.46	-	-	4.71	4.64	87.04	1.40	0.74	53.22	80274	671.35

Source: Percentage calculated from Government of India (1991), *Panchayati Raj Institution in India, 1991*. Ministry of Rural Development, New Delhi.

*1. Per capita income is obtained using 1991 census rural population figures for each state.

2. The average per panchayat is worked out based on the Number of Village Panchayats for the respective state as reported in Government of India (1991) op. cit.

3. The per capita receipts of states (col 13) are worked from statewise data on revenue and capital receipts given in RBI Bulletin, April 1992 deflated by 1991 census figures.

Note: AP and UP per capita income includes JRY grants. Per capita income is used in the sense of receipts and not with reference to national income.

Table 1B
Percentage Distribution of Income of Panchayati Raj Institutions at Middle Level (Block Level) of Different States

Sl. No.	States	Taxes and fees (%)	Remunerative enterprises assets (%)	Revenue from lands (%)	Share of Revenue (%)	Matching incentive grants (%)	Grants from Govts. (%)	Govt. loan/ grants for creating remuneration assets (%)	Other income (%)	Average per block (Rs. lakhs)
1.	Andhra Pradesh	-	-	-	2.76	-	96.64	-	0.60	39.78
2.	Gujarat	4.23	0.20	3.38	5.35	5.18	74.73	3.54	3.39	108.69
3.	Haryana	29.84	-	-	-	-	70.16	-	-	0.84
4.	Himachal Pradesh	96.23	-	3.77	-	-	-	-	-	0.82
5.	Madhya Pradesh	96.23	-	3.77	-	-	-	-	-	-
6.	Punjab	1.30	7.80	-	6.99	-	36.75	-	47.15	5.21
7.	Orissa	-	-	-	-	-	100.00	-	-	1.13
8.	Rajasthan	27.65	-	-	4.79	32.73	5.96	-	28.87	0.49
9.	Tamil Nadu	4.42	-	-	5.12	9.31	81.14	-	-	55.64
10.	Uttar Pradesh	46.23	-	-	-	-	47.83	-	5.93	2.67

Source: Percentage and column 11 are worked out from Government of India (1991): See Table 1a footnote.

Table 2
Own Resources and Grants of Maharashtra Zilla Parishads (1980-81 - 1988-89)

Sl No.	Year	Own resource (in- (cluding assigned resources	Total Government grants	Total resources	Percentage of own resources to total resources	Total free resources	Total free resources to total resources
(1)	(2)	(3)	(4)	(5)	(6) (Col: 3/Col: 5)	(7)	(8) (Col: 7/Col: 5)
1.	1980-81	16.64	260.04	276.68	5.9	25.58	9.8
2.	1981-82	17.06	287.52	304.58	5.6	26.97	9.3
3.	1982-83	18.42	336.34	354.76	5.2	28.87	8.6
4.	1983-84	17.16	391.33	408.49	4.2	30.06	7.4
5.	1984-85	20.39	476.16	496.55	4.1	37.47	7.4
6.	1985-86	24.57	557.75	582.32	4.2	40.75	7.4
7.	1986-87	27.67	558.41	586.08	4.7	43.65	7.4
8.	1987-88	32.02	658.96	690.98	4.6	52.75	7.7
9.	1988-89	32.94	761.91	794.85	4.1	59.32	7.4

(**Source**: Worked out from V. Ranganathan (1992) Table 1 and Table 2)

Appendix A: Table 1
Source-wise Income of Mandal Panchayats, 1987-88 to 1991-92 (in Rs)

Category of Income	1987-88	1988-89	1989-90	1990-91	1991-92	Total	Compound growth rate
HUNASANAHALLI MANDAL							
1. Tax Revenue	2204.66	36482.70	49119.30	37434.85	56393.50	181635.01	91.73
2. Non Tax Revenue	0.00	5214.00	13836.00	3740.00	4160.00	26950.00	-18.01
3. Others	8435.82	13243.00	7585.00	2125.15	1583.00	32971.97	-40.40
4. Grants from the govt.	73802.00	168725.00	108627.00	188523.65	106560.00	646237.65	8.82
a. Total	84442.48	223664.70	179167.30	231823.65	168696.50	887794.63	15.26
b. JRY Grant	N.A	N.A	534258.50	286317.90	498975.80	1319552.20	-3.36
Total of a+b	84442.48	223664.7	713425.80	518141.55	66672.30	2207346.83	64.47
JULAPALYA MANDAL							
1. Tax Revenue	13128.50	18780.75	20905.30	20385.10	6500.00	79699.65	-12.40
2. Non Tax Revenue	0.00	0.00	1135.00	8560.00	1238.00	10933.00	4.44
3. Others	10895.75	39124.25	2400.00	1070.00	12050.00	65540.00	-28.81
4. Grants from the govt.	69599.26	70658.00	76373.00	76745.00	75384.00	368759.26	2.45
a. Total	93623.51	128563.00	100813.30	106760.10	95172.00	524931.91	-1.52
b. JRY Grant	N.A	N.A	382650.90	162736.92	210481.77	755869.59	-25.83
Total of a+b	93623.51	128563.00	483464.20	269497.02	305653.77	1280801.50	36.43

Contd....

Appendix A: Table 1 Contd...

Category of Income	1987-88	1988-89	1989-90	1990-91	1991-92	Total	Compound growth rate
HINKAL MANDAL							
1. Tax Revenue	75359.19	421061.39	666585.44	1988650.33	3085888.17	6237544.52	145.40
2. Non Tax Revenue	13565.00	31389.00	71465.50	457251.00	1662921.00	2236591.50	242.00
3. Others	83966.14	54118.00	85092.00	207134.00	234135.30	664445.44	40.40
4. Grants from the govt.	89650.00	60000.00	230100.00	450240.85	446990.50	1276981.35	68.69
a. Total	262540.33	566568.39	1053242.94	3103276.18	5429934.97	10415562.81	117.26
b. JRY Grant	N.A	N.A	425271.00	324216.00	194601.60	944088.60	-32.35
Total of a+b	262540.33	566568.39	1478513.94	3427492.18	5624536.57	11359651.41	120.98
N. BELTUR MANDAL *							
1. Tax Revenue	20000.00	NA	62000.00	62000.00	112000.00	256000.00	50.56
2. Non Tax Revenue	3000.00	NA	88000.00	94000.00	67500.00	252500.00	127.37
3. Others	0.00	NA	56500.00	79000.00	62500.00	198000.00	5.18
4. Grants from the govt.	78652.00	NA	135500.00	135000.00	135000.00	484152.00	14.89
a. Total	101652.00	NA	342000.00	370000.00	377000.00	1190652.00	40.24
b. JRY Grant	NA	NA	404056.00	422273.35	317745.45	1144074.80	-11.32
Total a+b	101652	NA	746056	792273.35	694745.45	2334726.8	65.44

Contd...

Appendix A: Table 1 Contd...

	Category of Income	1987-88	1988-89	1989-90	1990-91	1991-92	Total	Compound growth rate
				BINAGA MANDAL				
1.	Tax Revenue	54390.65	63797.60	62540.70	69085.76	69817.36	319632.08	5.90
2.	Non Tax Revenue	7080.00	18686.80	32420.35	19474.20	50159.00	127820.35	48.54
3.	Others	1681.00	2740.00	1115.00	1032.35	577.00	7145.35	-26.76
4.	Grants from the govt.	78390.25	121627.35	52065.00	64148.00	94420.00	410650.60	-2.64
	a. Total	141541.90	206851.75	148141.05	153740.31	214973.36	865245.38	5.54
	b. JRY Grant	N.A	N.A	122507.00	75611.00	84409.00	282527.00	-16.99
	Total of a+b	141541.9	206851.75	270648.05	229351.313	299382.361	1147775.375	17.37
				KOPPA MANDAL				
1.	Tax Revenue	1234.08	3314.95	2381.15	3296.00	3022.00	13248.18	19.55
2.	Non Tax Revenue	500.00	0.00	600.00	2160.60	998.00	4258.60	29.49
3.	Others	4809.72	5762.20	4006.44	11795.44	3697.94	30071.74	1.92
4.	Grants from the govt.	21295.00	21802.10	38696.00	16096.00	40696.00	138585.10	10.43
	a. Total	27838.80	308779.25	45683.59	33348.04	48413.94	186163.62	12.57
	b. JRY Grant	N.A	N.A	32537.00	82817.00	0.00**	115354.00	154.53
	Total of a+b	27838.8	30879.25	78220.59	116165.04	48413.94	301517.62	27.53

Contd...

Appendix A: Table 1 Contd...

Category of Income	1987-88	1988-89	1989-90	1990-91	1991-92	Total	Compound growth rate
			SAGARA MANDAL				
1. Tax Revenue	20000.00	21000.00	22000.00	30000.00	35000.00	128000.00	15.90
2. Non Tax Revenue	10000.00	5000.00	10000.00	10000.00	45000.00	45000.00	7.18
3. Others	3000.00	4000.00	3000.00	5000.00	38000.00	53000.00	69.91
4. Grants from the govt.	79300.00	79300.00	79300.00	79300.00	79300.00	396500.00	0.00
a. Total	112300.00	109300.00	114300.00	124300.00	162300.00	622500.00	9.04
b. JRY Grant**	N.A.	N.A	-	-	-	-	-
Total of a+b	112300.00	109300.00	114300.00	124300.00	162300.00	622500.00	9.04
			TAJ SULTANPUR MANDAL				
1. Tax Revenue	22887.00	40963.00	98082.00	215978.00	443600.00	821510.00	113.64
2. Non Tax Revenue	45158.00	91428.00	86800.00	66300.00	103382.00	393068.00	14.28
3. Others	24736.00	6830.00	76750.00	38400.00	54750.00	201466.00	39.32
4. Grants from the govt.	70939.00	70939.00	168399.00	186127.00	73200.00	569604.00	10.82
a. Total	163720.00	210160.00	430031.00	506805.00	674932.00	1985648.00	44.96
b. JRY Grant	N.A	N.A	369980	279683	183792	833455.00	-29.52
Total of a+b	163720.00	210160.00	800011.00	786488.00	858724.00	2819103.00	58.95

Contd...

Appendix A: Table 1 Contd..

Category of Income	1987-88	1988-89	1989-90	1990-91	1991-92	Total	Compound growth rate
TOTAL OF ALL MANDALS							
1. Tax Revenue	209204.08	605400.39	983613.89	2426830.04	3812221.03	8037269.44	105.32
2. Non Tax Revenue	79303.00	151717.80	304256.85	661485.80	1900358.00	3097121.45	118.70
3. Others	137524.43	125817.45	236448.44	34556.94	407293.24	1252640.50	37.46
4. Grants from the govt.	561627.51	593051.45	889060.00	1196180.50	1051550.50	4291469.96	21.60
a Total	987659.02	1475987.09	2413379.18	4630053.23	7171422.77	16678501.35	66.67
b JRY Grant	N.A	N.A	2271260.40	1633655.17	1490005.62	5394921.19	-19.00
Total of a+b	987659.02	1475987.09	4684639.58	6263708.45	8661428.39	22073422.54	78.39

Note : N.A. Not Applicable/Applicable
* Information not available for 1988-89
** Information not available
Source: Aziz (1993a) pp. 63-64

Appendix A: Table 2
Percentage Share of Source-wise Income of Mandal Panchayats Including JRY Grants 1987-88 to 1991-92

	Category of Income	1987-88	1988-89	1989-90	1990-91	1991-92	Five Year Average
1.	Tax Revenue	21.18	41.02	21.00	38.74	44.01	36.41
2.	Non Tax Revenue	8.03	10.28	6.49	10.56	21.94	14.03
3.	Others	13.92	8.52	5.05	5.52	4.70	5.67
4.	Grants from the govt.	56.86	40.18	18.98	19.10	12.14	19.44
5.	JRY Grant	0.00	0.00	48.48	26.08	17.20	24.00

Note: N.A. Not Applicable
* Information not available for 1988-89
** Information Not Available.
Source: Aziz (1993a) pp67-68.

Appendix A: Table 3
Expenditure Pattern of Mandal Panchayats, 1987-88 to 1991-92
(Average of Seven Mandals including Hinkal)

	Category of Income	1987-88	1988-89	1989-90	1990-91	1991-92	Total
1.	Civic Amenities	28956.15 (40.45)	38427.19 (33.70)	66651.42 (33.79)	61575.99 (26.25)	62421.61 (25.60)	258032.37 (29.96)
2.	Public Works	13344.29 (18.64)	30913.70 (27.11)	56829.46 (28.81)	98820.89 (42.13)	79939.71 (32.78)	279848.05 (32.49)
3.	SC/ST Welfare	6700.00 (9.36)	7529.19 (6.60)	14704.29 (7.45)	25270.93 (10.77)	25918.57 (10.63)	80122.97 (9.30)
4.	Developmental Purpose	1619.29 (2.26)	3048.86 (2.67)	11035.71 (5.58)	1092.86 (0.47)	2071.43 (0.85)	18838.14 (2.19)
5.	Others	20965.04 (29.29)	34120.64 (29.92)	48058.45 (24.36)	47782.38 (20.37)	73505.48 (30.14)	224431.98 (26.06)
	Total	71584.76 (100.00)	114039.57 (100.00)	197249.34 (100.00)	234543.04 (100.00)	243856.81 (100.00)	861273.51 (100.00)

Source: Aziz, A (1993a).

Appendix A: Table 4
JRY Fund Expenditure Pattern among Six Mandals
(Excluding Taj Sultanpur), 1989-90 to 1991-92)

Sl. No	Category of Expenditure	1989-90	1990-91	1991-91	Total
1.	Creation of Economic assets	174127.25 (10.67)	133130.15 (9.18)	255439.90 (16.84)	562697.30 (12.24)
2.	Social Forestry	85457.60 (5.24)	27265.00 (1.88)	2947.50 (0.19)	115670.10 (2.52)
3.	Public Works	795419.65 (48.74)	942334.15 (64.99)	728824.35 (48.04)	2466578.15 (53.63)
4.	Social Amenities	422380.75 (25.88)	223435.90 (15.41)	454813.15 (29.98)	1100629.80 (23.93)
5.	Works under 20% for SC/STs	55689.00 (3.41)	98821.87 (6.82)	14620.00 (0.96)	169130.87 (3.68)
6.	Others	58970.90 (6.06)	24925.77 (1.72)	60462.00 (3.99)	184358.67 (4.01)
	Total	1632045.15 (100.00)	1449912.84 (100.00)	1517106.9 (100.00)	4599064.89 (100.00)

Note : Figures in Parantheses are percentages.
Source: Áziz, A (1993a).

Appendix B
Sources of Income of 11 Panchayats of Two Blocks of District Saharanpur (UP)

Sl. No	Sources	1990-91	1991-92	1992-93
1.	Taxes	66675.50 (30.08)	71675.50 (28.48)	86447.50 (35.84)
2.	Own enterprises assets or sale of product	95642.00 (43.15)	108613.00 (43.16)	91267.00 (37.84)
3.	Share of land revenue	59341.00 (26.77)	71372.00 (28.36)	63461.00 (26.31)
4.	Total Income of panchayats excluding JRY	221658.50 (100)	251660.50 100	241175.50 100
5.	Allocation of fund under JRY	765864.00	550533.21	823078.00
6.	Ratio of JRY funds to total resources of panchayat	77.55	68.63	77.34
7.	Total resources including JRY	987522.50	802193.50	1064253.50
8.	Average income per panchayat	89774.77	72926.68	96750.32

Note: Figures in Parantheses are percentages
Source: Mahi Pal (1994).

Appendix C: Table 1
Sources of revenue of Murshidabad Zilla Parishad 1990-91 to 1992-93

		(Amount (Rs. in Lakhs)		
Sl. No	Sources	1990-91	1991-92	1992-93
Own Income				
1.	Share of tax and cess received from state Govt.	0.80 (.07)	0.87 (.09)	11.50 (.86)
2.	Internal Source	28.60 (2.66)	14.19 (1.56)	5.63 (.42)
Government Grants				
3.	Incentive grant	5.85 (.54)	5.85 (.64)	--
4.	Grants for meeting Establishment Cost	42.11 (3.91)	40.31 (4.42)	38.00 (2.83)
5.	Fund for assigned work	883.96 (82.18)	798.84 (87.63)	1258.64 (93.80)
(a)	JRY	721.01 (67.03)	623.76 (68.43)	1203.44 (89.69)
(b)	Rural water supply	21.10 (1.96)	22.00 (2.41)	18.72 (1.39)
(c)	Various schemes for education including mass education, construction of school building operation Blak Bond etc.	51.78 (4.81)	16.62 (1.82)	-
(d)	Other miscellaneous	90.07 (8.37)	136.46 (14.97)	36.48 (2.72)
6.	District Plan	114.30 (10.63)	51.50 (5.65)	28.00 (2.09)
		1075.62	911.56	1341.77

Source : Murshidabad ZP Budget estimates for 92-93 to 94-95.

Appendix C: Table 2
Allotment of United Fund to PR Bodies for Development Purposes under District Plan Fund Scheme

Year	Allotment (in Rs. Lakhs)
1985-86	1653.00
1986-87	1218.35
1987-88	1527.73
1988-89	3333.98
1989-90	6347.80
1990-91	4914.63
1991-92	468.29
1992-93	154.21
1993-94	450.00
1994-95 (Upto 9/94)	2598.00

(Source: Dept of Planning: Government of West Bengal)

Appendix D
A State-wise Analysis of Taxes on Agricultural Sector*: 1965-66 to 1993-94

	1965-66	1970-71	1975-76	1980-81	1981-82	1982-83	1983-84	1984-85	1985-86	1986-88	1987-88	1993-94 (B.E)
West Bengal	810	512	1,337	972	755	604	5,222	9,601	14,515	15,574	19,512	33,920
	(6.8)	(4.0)	(4.8)	(1.9)	(1.2)	(1.0)	(6.8)	(10.3)	(12.9)	(12.8)	(13.5)	(6.59)
Assam	833	912	2,011	1,849	1,697	1,133	1,555	4,051	6,483	6,659	3,116	6,980
	(27.1)	(32.4)	(33.9)	(28.1)	(18.8)	(10.5)	(11.5)	(21.4)	(27.6)	(27.2)	(12.5)	(5.49)
Orissa	294	175	852	647	526	499	894	590	1,592	2,081	3,016	2,477
	(9.0)	(5.3)	(12.5)	(4.9)	(3.3)	(2.9)	(4.4)	(2.6)	(5.6)	(6.2)	(7.8)	(1.27)
Rajasthan	700	1,072	1,586	966	2,502	2,437	2,102	1,501	1,562	2,002	2,263	3,001
	(14.60	(17.7)	(12.1)	(4.2)	(8.0)	(6.3)	(4.80	(3.1)	(2.8)	(3.1)	(2.9)	(0.97)
Karnataka	715	627	1,011	1,775	1,788	1,418	1,827	1,442	1,475	1,937	2,873	3,400
	(11.8)	(6.2)	(4.3)	(3.7)	(3.0)	(2.1)	(2.4)	(1.6)	(1.4)	(1.60	(2.0)	(0.64)
Bihar	1,227	924	2,411	1,338	1,673	1,468	2,190	1,685	2,784	2,657	1,558	2,015
	(14.8)	(11.7)	(12.9)	(4.80	(5.0)	(3.9)	(5.0)	(3.6)	(4.8)	(4.0)	(2.0)	(0.47)
Kerala	492	443	1,073	1,450	1,199	1,435	1,790	2,502	2,666	2,240	1,656	5,200
	(9.8)	(6.5)	(6.7)	(4.3)	(3.2)	(3.3)	(3.7)	(4.0)	(3.6)	(2.8)	(1.8)	(1.82)
Uttar Pradesh	2,442	2,694	5,832	3,848	5,687	4,974	6,259	5,456	2,791	2,948	3,576	3,502
	(18.4)	(17.6)	(14.8)	(6.0)	(6.9)	(5.4)	(6.3)	(4.80	(2.2)	(2.3)	(1.8)	(0.43)
Madhya Pradesh	700	730	2,514	964	1,183	1,309	1,654	1,628	1,955	1,552	1,941	2,400
	(10.3)	(8.4)	(10.9)	(2.5)	(2.5)	(2.3)	(2.6)	(2.3)	(2.4)	(1.6)	(1.7)	(0.54)

Contd..

Appendix D Contd..

	1965-66	1970-71	1975-76	1980-81	1981-82	1982-83	1983-84	1984-85	1985-86	1986-88	1987-88	1993-94 (B.E)
Maharashtra	583 (3.8)	1,437 (5.60	3,463 (5.9)	3,400 (3.0)	4,355 (3.2)	5,801 (3.5)	5,283 (3.4)	5,053 (2.6)	3,746 (1.6)	3,026 (1.1)	4,974 (1.5)	4,857 (0.56)
Tamil Nadu	799 (7.7)	629 (4.2)	1,627 (5.1)	409 (0.6)	1,775 (2.1)	1,547 (1.4)	1,210 (1.1)	3,922 (3.0)	3,578 (2.3)	2,292 (1.3)	2,355 (1.3)	4,500 (0.78)
Gujarat	732 (10.9)	899 (8.3)	867 (3.7)	1,292 (2.4)	1,452 (2.2)	1,362 (1.8)	1,622 (1.8)	1,702 (1.70	1,725 (1.6)	2,114 (1.7)	1,883 (1.2)	3,600 (0.80)
Andhra Pradesh	1,412 (15.5)	2,118 (15.6)	5,188 (15.9)	3,623 (6.2)	3,810 (5.4)	3,009 (3.7)	2,111 (2.2)	2,148 (1.8)	2,123 (1.5)	1,311 (0.8)	1,624 (0.9)	3,273 (0.59)
Punjab	398 (5.6)	171 (2.0)	1,980 (1.5)	242 (0.7)	319 (0.7)	337 (0.7)	253 (0.5)	355 (0.6)	323 (0.5)	303 (0.6)	297 (0.3)	350 (0.15)
Haryana	--	199 (4.5)	774 (6.6)	510 (2.2)	449 (1.5)	460 (1.4)	471 (1.3)	395 (1.0)	379 (0.8)	233 (0.4)	53 (0.1)	170 (0.08)
All States	12,181 (10.9)	13,629 (8.9)	32,835 (9.3)	23,448 (3.5)	29,362 (3.6)	27,899 (2.9)	35,751 (3.3)	42,263 (3.5)	47,971 (2.8)	46,937 (2.8)	51,031 (2.6)	80,145 (1.18)

Notes: * Includes land revenue and agricultural income tax, surcharge on cash crops and cess and purchase tax on sugarcane wherever levied.
Figures within brackets show percentage to total tax revenue of the States.
Source: CMIE (1990) and RBI Bulletin, February 1994.

Appendix E
Grants for Panchayats
(Period 1996-97 to 1999-2000)

(Rs. Crores)

State	1996-97	1997-98	1998-99	1999-2000	1996-2000
1	2	3	4	5	6
Andhra Pradesh	87.75	87.75	87.75	87.75	351.00
Arunachal Pradesh	1.13	1.13	1.13	1.12	4.51
Assam	33.34	33.34	33.34	33.34	133.36
Bihar	126.80	126.80	126.79	126.80	507.19
Goa	1.48	1.48	1.48	1.47	5.91
Gujarat	48.00	48.00	48.00	48.01	192.01
Haryana	20.66	20.66	20.66	20.66	82.64
Himachal Pradesh	8.05	8.05	8.04	8.04	32.18
Jammu & Kashmir	9.40	9.40	9.40	9.39	37.59
Karnataka	55.44	55.44	55.44	55.45	221.77
Kerala	44.70	44.70	44.70	44.71	178.81
Madhya Pradesh	87.17	87.17	87.17	87.18	348.69
Maharashtra	86.75	86.75	86.75	86.76	347.01
Manipur	2.33	2.33	2.33	2.32	9.31
Meghalaya	2.16	2.16	2.17	2.16	8.65
Mizoram	0.74	0.74	0.73	0.73	2.94
Nagaland	1.16	1.16	1.16	1.17	4.65
Orissa	50.25	50.25	50.25	50.24	200.99
Punjab	25.84	25.84	25.84	25.83	103.35
Rajasthan	53.05	53.05	53.06	53.06	212.22
Sikkim	0.48	0.48	0.47	0.47	1.90
Tamil Nadu	71.83	71.83	71.84	71.84	287.34
Tripura	3.48	3.48	3.49	3.49	13.94
Uttar Pradesh	189.88	189.88	189.88	189.88	759.52
West Bengal	83.36	83.36	83.36	83.37	333.45
Grant Total	1095.23	1095.23	1095.23	1095.14	4380.93

Source: Report of the Tenth Finance Commission, p. 40).

Finance Commissions and Restructuring of Panchayat Finances

Abhijit Datta

THE paper is divided into two parts. Part I focuses on the tasks before the State Finance Commissions (SFCs) in relation to 'panchayat' functions and finances. Part II considers the issues relating to the fiscal restructuring of the 'panchayats' in terms of their plan finance and revenue base. Some of the generic issues relating to devolution of fiscal powers to the panchayats and strengthening of their fiscal position are also spelled out in the paper.

I

Rationalising Panchayat Functions

EXPENDITURE ASSIGNMENTS: The first task in fiscal reform of the panchayats is to rationalise their functional domain or expenditure assignments. A quick look at the conformity legislations from this angle reveals a confusing situation. Instead of rationalising the panchayat functions in terms of their 'exclusive,' ' state-concurrent' and agency responsibilities, the conformity legislations have provided for an additional dose of 29 items for the panchayats as indicated under the 11th Schedule of the 73rd Amendment.

The panchayat functions listed in these legislations usually run into more than 100 entries divided into compulsory and optional categories distributed haphazardly among the three or two tiers. However, if one relates these existing 'functions' to the 7th Schedule entries, the exclusive functions of the panchayats would be only two, and another 9 of these would be state-concurrent. Most of these functions relate to village-level civic services, while the agricultural, social and welfare services of the panchayats are usually undertaken on an agency basis. In effect, the functional jurisdiction of the panchayats is extremely narrow due to; (a) parallel local service provision by the states, and (b) assigning of only the 'maintenance tasks' to the panchayats for rural asset management.

The reasons for this unsatisfactory situation are not far to seek – under an arrangement of devolved decentralisation, only the inconsequential and residual functions have been allotted to the panchayats; this is now partly corrected under the indicative 11th Schedule list of desired panchayat functions, although some of these are not easily traceable to the 7th Schedule, and a few of these are objects of expenditure rather than functions. Article 243-G under the 73rd Amendment mentions panchayat functions in terms of 'plan preparation' and 'implementation of schemes,' although its specification of the panchayats as 'institutions of self-government' indicates a somewhat different functional role than what has been itemised under the 11th Schedule, especially for their civic responsibilities.

EXCLUSIVE AND CONCURRENT FUNCTIONS: For a clarity of panchayat functions it is necessary to identify their 'exclusive' spheres of activities where the benefit spill-overs do not cross local jurisdictions, and allocate these to the various tiers of panchayats according to their organisational capacities. Obviously, only the allocational responsibilities would be covered in this process, leaving the stabilisation and distributive aspects to be discharged by the central government.

However, some of the function-specific distributive activities could have panchayat participation in terms of delivery arrangements for targeted beneficiaries. These would be 'concurrent' panchayat functions. Also, the human development activities covering education and health care services may have to be organised at the local level with minimum service entitlements to be financed through specific grants to reflect state-wide and national priorities.

Appendix Table-1 attempts to differentiate the exclusive and concurrent functions indicated in the 73rd Amendment. It will be seen that only a-third of these could be regarded as exclusive, and the rest two-thirds are shown as concurrent panchayat functions. All functions related to support services to agriculture and allied activities are treated as concurrent, because these flow from the policy stance of the state governments to intervene in the private production processes. With a change in policy towards farm subsidy, most of these activities are likely to disappear. Panchayats have very little role in influencing such a policy process.

AGENCY FUNCTIONS: The policy of 'democratic centralism' of the panchayats initiated since the early '60s gave rise to the tendency to regard panchayati raj institutions (PRIs) as field agents of the states' functional departments. During the initial years of dismantling the community development set-up this was perhaps inevitable. But, unfortunately the tendency continued and the local government role of the panchayats was not allowed to flourish by the district administration which sustained and controlled them. To this were added the centrally-sponsored schemes for rural development which further strengthened the agency role of the PRIs. In many of the states panchayats are being used to perform only these agency tasks by the state and central governments. If the panchayats are to emerge as institutions of local self-government, as indicated under the 73rd Amendment, then this agency role is to be drastically reduced, confined only to occasional activities (like census, elections, disaster relief etc.) and undertaken voluntarily on contract.

PRIVATE PARTICIPATION: Allocation of functional responsibilities to the panchayats does not mean their monopoly over production of services, but only their role as providers of last resort so that their regulatory role is supposed to predominate over their producer role. Necessary legislative provisions are to be made to transform the future panchayats to act as facilitators and enablers so that private and non-governmental participation in the planning, financing, delivery and management of the various local services could be undertaken. The panchayats would, of course, be responsible for laying standards for each service, both quantitative and qualitative, and ensure the needs of the poor and protection of the environment. Such a move is already discernible for market oriented municipal services and for urban infrastructure.

From the angle of debureaucratisation, it is necessary for the panchayats to promote such partnership arrangements through contracting-out many of their functions and, where possible, consider outright privatisation of some of their activities, like collection of taxes and user charges. In human development services, with a number of agencies running schools and health care centres, distribution of vouchers to the eligible beneficiaries might be possible after the voter identity cards have been issued.

Designing Panchayat Finances

TASKS OF THE SFCs: The tasks facing the SFCs seem to be much more difficult than those of the Central Finance Commission (CFC) in that the SFCs are required to clarify panchayat functions and also evaluate their working before making their recommendations on a desired package of panchayat taxes, itemised revenue sharing and quantum of general grants. As already noted, the 11th Schedule functional approach is not very helpful in this regard – it is far too narrow in its implications for self-government, and far too wide in its functional involvement.

The first responsibility of the SFCs is to see that the existing panchayat activities are financed adequately, before exploring the possibility of suggesting devolution of additional functions as per the 11th Schedule, and then work out their fiscal and staff implications for both the state government and the panchayats in this regard. If the SFCs adopt the soft approach to confine their recommendations to those relating to the existing functions and leave the functional devolution entirely to the states, the constitutional requirement under Article 243-G will not be met. On the other hand, the states seem to have taken the position that the SFCs would suggest a fiscal additionality to the CFC to finance the 11th Schedule functions without making the states to part their own revenues.

This *impasse* needs to be broken. The only feasible alternative to the immediate down-sizing of the states due to additional functional devolution to the panchayats is to channelise the central assistance for the centrally-sponsored schemes on rural development to the panchayats to finance the

11th Schedule functions, with pass-through arrangement *via* the states. The future thrust of centrally-sponsored schemes for local government would have to be on promotion of only those local functions for which a minimum level of national standard needs to be fulfilled, such as, provision of drinking water, universalisation of primary education, primary health care for all, sheltering the poor etc. Of course, this is a matter on which the SFCs cannot take a decision; the future CFC will have to take a view in this matter.

TWO-STAGE EXERCISES: At the outset, the SFCs are required to determine the existing functional responsibilities of the panchayats and calculate the current revenue gap on the basis of forecasts of existing expenditure needs and prospects for own revenues. The subsequent exercise involves specification of the revenue implications for newly devolved functions on the basis of current expenditure for these functions, and projecting these to meet the future requirements of the panchayats. The combined revenue gap for the existing and devolved panchayat functions would then require marginal revenue additionality to what is already subsumed in the state and panchayat budgets. This does involve staff redundancy at the state-level which needs to be solved separately by the state government.

Down-sizing the Upper-level Governments

Panchayat level decentralisation involves contraction of the machinery of the state government, its field set-up and the functional parastatals along with the devolution process. Similar reorganisation of the central machinery is also involved when it shares a a part of its tax revenues for the local governments. Local decentralisation entails shrinkage of the upper-level governments – for the states due to functional devolution, and for the centre due to future central tax-sharing and reduction of central schemes for local governments. The conventional adage that local-level decentralisation prospects are limited by resource constraints is not correct; the problem lies in avoiding the down-sizing of the upper-level governments involving their surplus staff.

Financing Devolved Functions

A FISCAL DEVOLUTION PACKAGE: *Appendix* Table-2 presents a package of fiscal devolution to the panchayats by adopting a middle position. It attempts; (a) considerable increase in panchayats' own activities for both exclusive and concurrent functions, and (b) indicates a range of taxes that could be either wholly assigned to or shared with the panchayats so as to reduce the load on the general grants. The explicit objective is to finance at least a-half of panchayat functions – both exclusive and concurrent – from their own taxes and shared tax revenues, as in the case of the states.

It will be noticed that the own taxes of the panchayats have either fixed or local tax bases; similarly, the shared taxes also have predominantly local bases, making these amenable for allocation on derivative principles. The specific grants are to be kept outside the purview of the block grant calculations; similarly, the cost reimbursement arrangements for the agency activities of the panchayats are contractual in nature and, hence, outside the scheme of fiscal devolution to the panchayats.

THE GENERAL GRANT: The general grant to the panchayats may have to be given only to the Zilla Panchayat, so that the budgets of the other two lower tiers could be financed from their own revenues, shared taxes and specific grants. This is to be achieved over a period of the first 10 years after the constitution of the newly elected panchayats and transferring some of their functions to the next higher tier panchayats for balancing their budgets. During the transition period, the upper tier panchayat may assist the concerned Anchal and Gram Panchayats to meet their budgetary deficits. This will not conflict with the objectives of decentralisation so long as the aggregate fiscal devolution to the panchayats is positive.

The same strategy of transferring back some of the Zilla Panchayat functions to the states may be adopted over a 10-year period to see that the general grants do not cover more than a-half of Zilla Panchayat expenditures; at the same time, the revenue expenditure of the Zilla Panchayats should reach at least a-fifth of state revenue expenditure, so that the fiscal responsibility objectives for the Zilla Panchayats are matched by a corresponding fiscal decentralisation commitment on the part of the states. These percentages are, of course, notional; but they do point out the need to balance the two conflicting fiscal strategies.

If the design of fiscal decentralisation for the panchayats is made to work, then the *inter-se* distribution of the general grants could be made to correct horizontal imbalances among the Zilla Panchayats to pull up the below-average authorities to the standards of unit cost of expenditure for various functions and that of tax efforts of the average performer. This means that the general grant to the panchayats is to be formula-based and applied separately for each of the three tiers of the PRIs. On the other hand, vertical fiscal disabilities of the individual units of the panchayats are to be ensured through development assistance weighted for the backward districts. The primary task of the SFCs is to correct horizontal, rather than vertical, imbalances of the panchayats.

Generic Issues of Fiscal Transfer

DATA BASE: Given the absence of aggregative fiscal data on the panchayats and inadequate data base for the municipalities, the basic work of the SFCs would be to provide meaningful and complete fiscal data on local governments, using the accounting formats and budgetary heads of the state and central governments as provided by the Comptroller and Auditor-General (CAG). However, the tax and expenditure classifications of the local authorities may need fine tuning to be meaningful in local contexts, particularly for detailed expenditure heads. For this, the individual states may adopt further downward classifications, so that inter-state comparisons may still be made on the basis of the CAG formats. There is a need to publish this data regularly for use by all concerned.

LEGAL SPECIFICATION OF REVENUE SHARING: An alternative to the finance commission approach of determining the divisible revenue pool for distribution among the recipient governments is to constitutionally specify the entitlement of the total tax revenues of the donor government by the user governments. This approach has been suggested recently by the

10th CFC in the context of centre-state fiscal relations, and this is equally relevant in the context of state-local fiscal relations. In both Brazil and Nigeria – the other two Third World federations with constitutionally recognised local government – this approach has been used. Its drawback is dilution of fiscal responsibility and accountability on the part of the recipients, but due to its certainty the central and state finance commissions are relieved of the unmanageable task of determining the size of ever increasing sharable revenue pool.

In the context of SFCs it would perhaps be better to adopt a middle course by specifying the percentage of state revenues for the panchayats and the municipalities in the ratio of their relative expenditures as a substitute of future shared taxes and general grants. As a starter, a 30% sharing of states' own tax revenues may be adopted through legislative provision – of which about 10% could be the share of the panchayats.

Central Contribution

The issue of central government's contribution towards local-level decentralisation would have to be faced after the first round of the SFCs are over, so that the CFC will have to suggest the central contribution in terms of fiscal instrumentalities and purposes. If the objective is to smoothen the process of fiscal decentralisation, then tax sharing would be the preferred method. If, however, the central government wants to promote national objectives through local government activities in preferred directions of its choice, then specific grants would be more appropriate.

As noticed earlier, there is a danger of substituting local expenditure priorities by central priorities, as in the case of the existing rural development programmes. A wiser course would be to fold up these programmes, barring those for which a minimum national standard has been fixed, and route the same assistance through sharing of the most elastic central tax, i.e central excise. This assistance could be regarded as the 'own revenues' of the local bodies for the purpose of SFC-determined general grants on condition that the existing fiscal transfer commitments by the states are not reduced.

Similar condition exists in Australia for distribution of a share of central income tax to the local governments passed through the states.

The second aspect of central assistance pertains to the special category states. Instead of assisting them to the extent of 90% of their revenue expenditure, it is time that a part of this assistance, say 30%, is earmarked for their local governments. There is also a need to adopt similar approaches towards fiscal decentralisation for the local governments as well as for the autonomous districts and area councils within the same state. From this angle, the SFCs may have to be given additional responsibilities for harmonising fiscal federalism within a state in future.

Future Decentralisation Strategies

SHORT-TERM STRATEGIES: The immediate action strategies would include identification of the exclusive and state-concurrent functions of the local governments by the SFCs and that of their sources of finance from own revenues and transfers. Without unscrambling the expenditure assignments, it is futile to work out the revenue implications for fiscal transfer purposes. The SFCs must take a lead in this direction and should not wait for the states to follow the decentralisation requirements inherent in the 73rd Amendment.

An alternative route of revenue devolution through tax-sharing and general grants is a legal specification of sharing the tax revenues of the states for financing panchayat functions. If this route is preferred, then the states would be forced to specify the functional domain of the panchayats more clearly than they do at present for fear of losing their revenues and staff for the new functions indicated in the 11th Schedule to be devolved to the panchayats.

The central government has to decide, on the advice of the future CFC, whether to assist the panchayats through specific grants or sharing of its excise revenues. Tax-sharing has the advantage of being neutral in its effect on local expenditure priorities; however, specific grants also are meant to promote local functions having national priorities. Perhaps a combination of the two approaches may be acceptable in the present context. The central government should also decide whether a part of its revenue support to the special category states should be directed to the newly elected local governments.

MEDIUM-TERM STRATEGIES: In the medium-term, the SFCs are to see that the normal revenue expenditures of the sub-district panchayats are met from their own revenues and shared-taxes so that there may not be a need to finance their revenue deficit from the higher tier panchayats. The Zilla Panchayat budget may ultimately have to be kept in balance by transferring back some of their allotted functions, provided this does not disturb the pace of decentralisation.

In order to achieve fiscal decentralisation in a meaningful manner, it would be prudent for the SFCs to adopt state targets of tax devolution, while for the CFC a national public expenditure target for local government decentralisation might be more appropriate to decide about the quantum of fiscal assistance to the local governments.

COMMON STRATEGIES: Application of the twin tax devolution and public expenditure targets to the panchayats would largely correct the vertical fiscal imbalances among the three levels of government, while measures for horizontal fiscal disabilities could be taken within the three tiers of the PRIs. Vertical fiscal disabilities within the panchayats needs to be corrected through the development process outside the SFC-CFC mechanism.

II

Panchayats and Plan Finance

FISCAL DESIGN: The fiscal design of the panchayats flows from their role specification. The widely prevalent view that the panchayats are primarily agents for plan expenditure within their jurisdictions has inhibited their emergence as financially viable entities, or as a system of local self-government consisting of all their three tiers.

The 73rd and 74th Constitutional Amendments have not materially altered the situation in viewing the panchayats and the municipalities as 'institutions of self-government' having responsibilities for preparation of plans and implementation of schemes. Taken together, this enjoins both the panchayats and the municipalities to be largely self-reliant institutions of local government for undertaking community services and local infrastructure facilities. The so-called 'agency role' of the panchayats has to undergo drastic changes to fit into the fiscal requirements of autonomy, accountability, and transparency necessary for institutions of self-government to be operational.

PLAN ASSISTANCE FLOWS: Currently the entire plan budget of the panchayats consists of plan assistance from the central and state governments by way of sponsored schemes and projects. The largest of these is the Integrated Rural Development Programme (IRDP) – a centrally sponsored scheme under the central Ministry of Rural Development – and managed through district-level societies called 'District Rural Development Authorities' (DRDA). The DRDAs are creatures of the state government, but the funds are kept separate for operational purposes.

Apart from the IRDP, there are a number of other centrally-sponsored schemes and parts of central assistance to the state plan which find their way to the panchayats *via* district-level plan allocations, with or without modification of the original schematic loan-grant mix. The role of the state government in thus allocating plan finance to the panchayats is that of an intermediary since very little of the states' own resources are passed on to the panchayats. The IRDP funds constitute around 70% of plan budget of the panchayats in a typical district, and the rest 30% constitute reconditioned transfer of a part of central assistance for the state plan spent through the panchayats.

Fiscal Distortions

The most serious distortion arising from 100 % financing of the panchayat plan budget from the central and state resources is that the panchayat revenues have no linkages with their plan expenditure, which are supported by the central and state revenue bases. Even with zero revenue, the panchayats would be able to undertake their plan schemes in terms of functional priorities, expenditure norms and staffing patterns fixed by the donor governments. The first casualty of this arrangement of external financing of the panchayat plans is their fiscal accountability.

The second problem of externally-aided panchayat plans is the associated maintenance gap in their revenue budget for the non-IRDP schemes. Meeting such maintenance burden may entail serious distortions of local expenditure priorities, apart from perpetual dependence on state subventions to meet the revenue deficits of increased panchayat plan budgets. Consequently, this results in a loss of fiscal autonomy on the part of the panchayats, arising out of their external fiscal bondage.

The composition of plan assistance to the panchayats is the third problem in their fiscal system. The loan-grant mix of plan assistance to the panchayats may be more realistic than for the state plans, but this is basically notional. The loan component is not assessed in terms of the credit-rating of the separate panchayat units, nor is there any requirement of self-liquidation of financially viable assets. Basically, plan loans constitute a part of the directed credit which is slated for gradual abolition with the deepening of the financial sector reforms.

Inter-governmental plan assistance to the panchayats in future would consist of capital grants for ensuring their allocational equity and balancing central-local priorities with or without matching provisions. This implies the need for increased reliance on revenue mobilisation by the panchayats for own capital outlay, and also for servicing market loans. For the present, attempts are to be made to establish direct contact of the panchayats with public financial institutions for borrowings.

Panchayats and Non-Plan Finance

PLAN AND NON-PLAN FINANCE: The liberal transfer of plan assistance to the 'panchayats' has resulted in a hiatus between their plan and non-plan finances with consequential loss of fiscal autonomy and accountability. Financial health of any organisation is assessed in terms of its revenue flow and the size of its investment ought to be determined by its revenue capacity. A conventional ratio between the revenue and capital investments would be around 10:1, which assumes a 10 per cent surplus in the revenue budget for financing the capital investments. This ought to prevail over a medium term even in government, so as to avert financial bankruptcy. This simple rule has not been respected in India due to the adoption of Soviet-style plan financing.

In the panchayats the revenue-capital ratio would be the reverse of the indicated financial management norm, with the consequence of under-provision of operating expenditure, or shifting this responsibility to the field administration of the states, or a combination of both. Another way of looking at the arrangement is inadequate decentralisation of operating responsibility to the panchayats, and their excessive involvement in the disbursement of plan expenditures.

This is in sharp contrast to the situation in the municipalities where their revenue budgets show nominal surpluses with limited availability of state plan funds, but entails transfer of maintenance burden of assets created by the area development authorities. In the case of the states also there is an imbalance between their revenue and plan budgets, but this is not in such an absurd degree as in the panchayats. An immediate objective could be to bring about the same ratio of non-plan and plan finance in the panchayats as exists in the state government.

STRENGTHENING NON-PLAN FINANCE: The key to strengthening the non-plan finance of the panchayats lies in the pace of withdrawal of the states' field administration for local tasks. Such tasks constitute anywhere between 30-50% of the states' budget and are mostly spent on the salaries of district and sub-districts functionaries performing panchayat tasks. Compared to the combined non-plan expenditure of the panchayats in a district, the combined non-plan expenditure of the corresponding departments would be at least 100-fold. Even if 50% of such district non-plan allocation is transferred to the panchayats, the imbalance in their plan and non-plan budgets would be corrected considerably. This entails transferring the bulk of the district and sub-district functionaries of the state to the panchayats as was attempted in Karnataka panchayats in the mid-'80s.

However, this requires the states' field administration to function within the institutional cover of the panchayats, by severing the states' departmental linkages so that the panchayats could emerge as autonomous decision-making units. The states' functional interests effectively prevent such a decentralisation strategy for their own survival. The states' functional route to decentralisation thus becomes a non-starter unless measures for revenue decentralisation are attempted simultaneously.

Debureaucratisation

In the context of panchayat decentralisation, there are three senses in which debureaucratisation is called for. Firstly, this is to be applied during the process of internalisation of the field administration bureaucracy into the panchayats. Assuming a fat content in the states' field administration, the panchayats could do with a much lesser staff strength than what would be offered to them for absorption. Additionally, with a merger of different functional areas at the panchayat level, the same functionaries could be used for a multiplicity of tasks.

The second aspect of debureaucratisation of the panchayats relates to the direct involvement of their elected members in executive tasks, particularly those assigned to the various functional and local constituency committees. This is the classic British concept of debureaucratisation through local government involvement in public services.

The third sense of debueaucratisation is the strengthening of the institutions of civil society involving alternative non-governmental and private organisations to undertake specific local functions through contracting-out or even divestiture of public responsibilities. In an era of economic liberalisation, this aspect of panchayat debureaucratisation assumes particular significance. This is the neo-classical concept of local governance that goes beyond the creation of a local state and involves the citizens directly in the provision of community services.

From the angle of fiscal transfer there are two requirements to promote panchayat debureaucratisation: (a) direct staff assistance or salary reimbursement to the 'panchayats' should be replaced by measures for their revenue strengthening, and (b) specific grants should cover non-salary items of expenditure to promote debureaucratic measures by the panchayats.

An Agenda for Fiscal Reforms

STRENGTHENING REVENUE BASE: The future agenda for fiscal reform of the panchayats should include measures to strengthen their revenue base, such that their revenue budget can sustain the load of their plan budget. This would mean cutting down the size of plan assistance to the panchayats, particularly those components which are geared to meet national or state priorities of development. In the process, the limited role of the panchayats as instruments of rural development will be replaced by their generic status as institutions of self-government. Rural development is too broad a concern for any single level of government to meet.

FUNCTION-FINANCE NEXUS: The second requirement of fiscal reform of the panchayats is to link their revenue capabilities with the actual functions identified for decentralisation at the various tiers in terms of a particular tier (exclusive), for all the tiers (joint) and with the state government (concurrent). Separate revenue instrumentalities – like, new tax authority, shared and assigned state taxes, general and specific grants, expenditure reimbursement etc. – are to be used to meet the varied functional requirements of the panchayats. This means that the erstwhile Karnataka model of bureaucratic decentralisation should be avoided and the earlier Maharashtra-Gujarat model of autonomous panchayats is to be created. The consequential staff redundancy problem of the state government needs to be tackled separately.

MARKET BORROWING: The third requirement of panchayat fiscal reform is to reorient them to be self-reliant in their plan outlay so that they are able to source loans from the market. It is likely that only the zilla panchayats would be able to do this, so that the plan component of the lower tiers of the panchayats would consist of capital grants from the zilla panchayat and the state government.

EARNMARKING OF PLAN ASSISTANCE: The fourth requirement of panchayat fiscal reform is to create a separate local sector in the state plans and also in the centrally sponsored schemes. It is expected that in future the central government participation would be more in terms of general revenue assistance for the panchayats and promoting matters of national importance. The existing central schemes for the panchayats need reorientation so that there is no substitution of local responsibility in meeting national and regional tasks.

CONSTITUENCY ACCOUNTABILITY: The fifth requirement of panchayat fiscal reform is to reorient their financial management system to be largely self-regulating and accountable to their constituents, rather than to their upper tiers or to the state bureaucracy at different levels. State controls are to be exercised mainly though a system of incentives and disincentives, rather than through executive exercise of penal powers. This aspect has not so far attracted the attention of fiscal reformers, but the operative aspects of panchayat autonomy and accountability largely depend on the management reorientation of the panchayats after their capacity-building phase is over.

Conclusions

There are four broad conclusions emerging from our discussion of fiscal reforms of the panchayats:

(i) the panchayats are to be strengthened as institutions of self-government, and not merely as agents of state plan implementation;

(ii) the fiscal strengthening of the panchayats involves simultaneous measures for fiscal and organisational contraction of the state government;

(iii) the state field staff transfer strategy to the panchayats prevents fiscal decentralisation to take root; and

(iv) fiscal accountability of the panchayats is to be outside state bureaucratic control and related mainly to their constituents.

Appendix: Table 1
Desired Panchayat Functions: Exclusive and State Concurrent

Sl. No.	Desired Functions	Tiers	Constitutional Schedules 7th	11th
Exclusive Functions				
1.	Social and farm forestry	AP, GP	(III/17A)	(6)
2.	Minor forest produce	AP, GP	(II/19)	(7)
3.	Khadi, village & cottage industries	ZP, GP, AP	(II/24)	(9)
4.	Drinking water	ZP, AP, GP	(II/17)	(11)
5.	Fuel & fodder	AP, GP	(III/17A)	(12)
6.	Adult and non-formal education	ZP, AP, GP	(II/11)	(19)
7.	Libraries	ZP, AP, GP	(II/12)	(20)
8.	Cultural activities	ZP, AP, GP	(?)	(21)
9.	Markets & fairs	ZP,AP, GP	(II/28)	(22)
10.	Maintenance of community assets	ZP, AP, GP	(II/35)	(29)
Concurrent Functions				
1.	Agriculture, incl. agr. extension	ZP, AP, GP	(II/14)	(1)
2.	Land improvement, land reforms etc.	ZP, AP, GP	(II/18)	(2)
3.	Minor irrigation etc.	ZP, AP	(II/17)	(3)
4.	Animal husbandry, dairying & poultry	ZP, AP, GP	(II/15)	(4)
5.	Fisheries	ZP, AP, GP	(II/21)	(5)
6.	Small scale industries etc.	ZP, AP	(II/24)	(8)
7.	Rural housing	ZP, AP	(?)	(10)
8.	Roads, culverts, bridges, ferries, water ways etc.	ZP, AP, GP	(II/13)	(13)
9.	Rural electrification	ZP	(III/38)	(14)
10.	Non-conventional energy	ZP, AP	(?)	(15)
11.	Poverty alleviation	ZP, AP, GP	(?)	(16)
12.	Primary & secondary education	ZP, AP, GP	(II/11)	(17)
13.	Technical training & voc. education	ZP, AP	(III/25)	(18)
14.	Health & sanitation etc.	ZP, AP, GP	(II/6)	(23)
15.	Family welfare	ZP, AP	(III/20A)	(24)
16.	Women & child development	ZP, AP	(?)	(25)
17.	Social welfare etc.	ZP, AP	(III/23)	(26)
18.	Welfare of the weaker sections, esp. for SC/ST	ZP, AP, GP	(?)	(27)
19.	Public distribution system	ZP, AP, GP	(III/33)	(28)
20.	Economic & social planning	ZP	(III/23)	(-)

Appendix: Table 2
Desired Panchayat Revenue Sources for Exclusive and Concurrent Functions

Revenues	Gram Panchayats	Anchal Panchayats	Zilla Panchayats
(a) Own Resources			
1. Taxes	- Poll tax - Show tax	- Property tax - Service taxes - Show tax - Toll	- Professions tax - Octroi or its alternatives - Toll
2. Non-tax Revenues			
- Fees & User charges	- Various	- Various	- Various
- Property income	- "	- "	- "
3. Shared Taxes	- Land rate - Stamp duty - Electricity duty	- Land revenue - Stamp duty - Electricity - duty	- Entertainment Tax - Motor vehicle tax
(b) Transfers			
1. General Grants	- No	- No	- No
2. Specific Grants	- Various	- Various	- Various

INDEX

A

Administrative costs, 4
Andhra Pradesh, 4
Arabinda Ghosh, 17
Article - 243, 4
Article - 243 ZD, 2, 3, 21, 28
Article - 243 ZE, 2
Article - 243 I, 26
Article - 280 (bb), 3
Article - 280 (c), 2, 3
Assigned revenues, 5
Asoka Mehta Committee (1978), 5, 9
Australia, 63
Aziz, A., 13, 16

B

Bankala, 12
Bankruptcy, 67
Beneficiary Committee, 17
Bihar, 11, 20, 32
Bonds, 32
Budget, 21, 64
Budhadeb Ghosh, 17
Brazil, 62

C

CAARD, 32
CAARD Report (1985), 23
Capital Account, 24
Capital Expenditure, 24
Capital Grants, 24
Capital Investment, 67
Central Finance Commission, 58, 62, 63, 64
Cess, 6, 7, 10, 14, 20
Cess on Land Revenue, 7
Centre for Earth Sciences, 17
Civil Society, 69
Community Development Programme, 17
Comptroller and Auditor General, 60, 61
Concurrent, 56, 60, 169
Conformity Acts, 18, 19, 21, 22, 20
Consolidated Fund, 3

D

Datta. A, 9
Debentures, 32
Debureaucratisation, 68, 69
Decentralized Planning, 3, 22
Democratic decentralisation, 2, 33
Denmark, 9
District Equalisation Fund, 8, 21, 20
District Industries Centre, 2
District Planning Committee, 24
District Rural Development Agency, 2

E

Eleventh Schedule, 2, 55, 56, 19, 58, 63
Equalisation Grants, 7
Emmanuel Jimenez, 32
Entertainment Tax, 5, 6
Establishment Grants, 7
Estate Duty, 27
Exclusive Function, 56, 60
Exclusive ties, 69
Expenditure, 70

F

Fees, 5, 6, 14, 70
Fiscal Autonomy, 17, 25
Fiscal Discipline, 17, 25
Fiscal Decentralisation, 61, 63, 64
Fiscal Distortion, 66
Fiscal Federalism, 7
Flow of Funds, 5

G

Gadgil Formula, 28, 30
Girglani, J. M, 16, 28
Government of India (1963), 4
Government of India (1966), 18
Government of India (1978), 6, 9
Government of Karnataka (1989 a), 13
Gram Panchayats, 5, 6
Gram Panchayat Finance, 12
Grants, 5, 7, 8, 10, 11, 12, 14, 15, 26, 32, 60, 69, 70

Grants in aid, 12, 20, 25, 33
Gujarat, 8, 10, 11, 12, 19, 20, 21

H

Haryana, 7, 11, 19, 21, 31
Henry Maddick (1970), 18
Himachal Pradesh, 5, 12, 19, 20, 21
Hinkal Panchayat, 13
Hirsch W.Z. (1970), 7
House Tax, 5

I

Incentive grants, 7
Income Tax, 27, 63
Incremental budgeting, 31
Institutional Finance, 11
Institutions of Self-Government, 2, 32, 56, 65, 71
Integrated Rural Development Programme (IRDP), 3, 65, 66
Inter-governmental transfers, 22, 26
IDA, 17

J

JRY, 9, 13, 14, 15, 16

K

Karnataka, 5, 12, 13, 14, 16, 19 20, 29, 68
Karnataka Act 1985, 20
Kerala, 6,7,11
Kerala Sastra Sahitya Parishad, 17

L

Land revenue, 6, 7, 20
Loans, 5, 21, 24, 70
Local Area Development Scheme, 3

M

Madhya Pradesh, 8, 9, 11, 12, 17, 19,21
Maddick, H., 17
Maharashtra, 5, 7, 10, 11, 14, 15 16, 17, 19, 20
Mahi Pal, 16, 17
Mandal Panchayat, 12, 13, 29
Maintenance tasks, 56
Matching grants, 7
Meenakshisundaram, S. S, 3
Metropolitan committee, 3
Million Well Scheme, 17
Ministry of Agriculture, 23, 32
Multi-level Public Finance, 4
Murshidabad, 14

N

Narasimham Committee (1981), 6
Narayana Rao, K.V. (1981), 6
Nayantara, 17
Nigeria, 62
Non-IRDP, 66
Non-plan budget, 68
Non-plan finance, 67,68
Non-tax revenue,
Non-plan expenditure, 68

O

Orissa, 12

P

Panchayat Finance Corporation, 11, 32
Panchayat Samiti, 5, 16, 7
Panchayat Samiti Finance, 11
Panchayat Raj Bodies, 7
Pande, A. K, 12
Per capita expenditure, 24
Per capita income, 9
Per capita receipts, 9, 11
Per panchayat income, 9
Performance Budgetary, 32
Philippines, 32
Pilgrim tax, 5
Planning Commission, 3, 17, 23, 24, 28
Plan Budget, 67
Profession tax, 5
Pradhan, 13
Public contribution, 11
Public expenditure, 64
Punjab, 7, 11, 19, 20

R

Rafiq Zakaria Committee (1963), 17
Rajasthan, 10, 11, 12, 21, 29
Remunerative enterprises, 5
Report of Tenth Finance Commission (1994), 23

Revenue account, 24
Revenue budget, 66, 67, 69
Revenue flow, 67
Revenue capacity, 67
Revenue-capital ratio, 67
Revenue expenditure, 63
Revenue investment, 67
RBI Bulletin, 17

S

Saharanpur, 14, 16
Salaries, 68, 69,
Santhanam Committee Report(1963), 4, 9
73rd Amendment, 1, 2, 5, 4, 23, 28, 29, 55, 56, 57, 63, 65
74th Amendment, 1, 2, 21, 28, 29,
Seventh Schedule, 55, 56
Shyamali, 17
Sirmaur, 12
Sikkim, 19
Soviet style plan financing, 67
Spatial planning, 28
State Council, 20
State Equalisation Fund, 7, 20
State Finance Commission, 21, 22, 23, 26, 27, 29, 30, 33, 55, 58, 59, 60, 62, 63,64
State Government, 55
State legislations, 7
Structure of panchayat finance, 5
Surcharges, 6
Surcharges on stamp duty, 7

T

Taxes, 5, 6, 7, 10, 14, 20, 21, 26, 29, 30, 31, 60, 61, 70
Tax on agricultural land, 5
Tax on animals, 5
Tax revenue, 59, 60
Tamil Nadu, 6, 7, 11, 12, 20
Tenth Finance commission, 23, 26, 27, 62
Thavaraj, M. J. K.(1978), 27
Toll, 6, 10, 20
Total government expenditure, 8
Twin taxes, 64

U

Union Government, 2
UNDP, 9, 4
Union Finance Commission, 22, 23, 24, 26, 29
U.P, 5, 9, 11, 12,1 4, 15, 16, 17, 20, 32
U.P. State Planning Institute, 16

V

Vehicle tax, 5

W

Wallace E Oats (1991), 30
West Bengal, 5, 10, 16, 17, 20, 31

Z

Zero base budgeting, 32
Zilla Parishad, 5, 6, 7, 15, 16
Zilla Parishad finances, 14